MYTHS OF ANCIENT GREECE AND ROME

Editor: John Holdren

Assistant Editor: Vanessa Wright

Art Director: Steve Godwin

Designer: Jayoung Cho

ISBN: 1-931728-49-6

Printed by Worzalla, Stevens Point, WI, USA, March 2011, LOT 032011

TABLE OF CONTENTS

GREEK MYTHS:
WINDOWS ON A LOST WORLD

Imagine you could open a window and look through the dim mists of time to a lost world, more than two thousand years in the past. You would see a people so fierce that three hundred soldiers hold off an army of thousands, and yet, at the same time, a people so thoughtful that they choose to rule themselves rather than submit to being ruled by a king. In this world, a city of white marble, dedicated to wisdom, shines like a beacon by the sea.

This was the world of the ancient Greeks. There, on a sunny peninsula in southern Europe, surrounded by the clear blue waters of the Mediterranean Sea, ideas and principles were forged that still shape our modern world. The Greeks loved learning, reason, and freedom of thought. Greek ideas of citizenship and democracy remain some of our most cherished values. Ancient Greek art and literature are still studied and enjoyed today.

One window through which you may look back to the world of the ancient Greeks is by way of the stories they told. These stories describe the world as the Greeks saw it, and as they dreamed it might be. In these stories, the Greeks explained what they thought made a person a hero, a true friend, or a fool. They showed what it meant to be Greek, and what it meant to be human.

We call these stories myths, and through them, we get a glimpse of the ancient Greeks through their own eyes. In these myths, you will meet ordinary people, heroes, monsters, and a family of mighty beings the Greeks called their gods and goddesses. The Greeks believed that these beings caused everything that happened in their world. They believed that every flash of lightning, every springtime crop, every autumn harvest, and every sunset glow was the work of one of the gods or goddesses.

The king of these gods, the most powerful of them all, was called Zeus. The Greeks imagined him as a tall, strong man with long hair and a flowing beard. They said it was he who judged between quarreling gods, and, when angry, spoke in thunder and hurled lightning bolts across the sky. His wife, Hera, was the queen of the gods. She was tall and beautiful, with golden hair and blazing eyes. But while she could be charming and kind, if crossed, she became bitter and vengeful.

Athena and Aphrodite were two of Zeus's daughters. Gray-eyed Athena, the goddess of wisdom, was noble and brave. Aphrodite, the goddess of love, was so beautiful that

vengeful: strongly desiring to punish or get back at someone

everyone who looked at her loved her. You may have heard of Aphrodite's son, Eros, who is also called Cupid, a rascal whose arrows caused gods and men alike to fall in love with the next person they met, no matter how much trouble it might cause.

Hermes was one of Zeus's sons. Whenever Zeus wished to send news, Hermes, wearing his winged cap and sandals, would bear the message, as quick as thought, to its destination. He often carried with him a caduceus, a messenger's staff crowned with wings, around which two snakes were twined.

Zeus also had two brothers: Poseidon and Hades. Poseidon was the ruler of the sea. When he was pleased, the waters were still and calm. But when he grew angry, the ocean floor shook with his rage and churned up terrible waves. Hades, though, showed little such emotion. Neither joy nor anger stirred the cold heart of the grim ruler of the underworld, the dark regions underneath the earth where, the Greeks believed, people went when they died.

The Greeks believed that many of these gods lived on a snow-capped peak called Mount Olympus, where they gathered from time to time in Zeus's banquet hall to discuss the affairs of men. The Greeks also believed that the gods and goddesses sometimes came down from Mount Olympus to walk among people on earth, helping those they favored, and punishing the wicked. Their help might come in the form of a gift, such as strong armor and a sturdy shield, or a solution to a problem. Punishment might mean turning a person into an animal to teach him a lesson, or causing a storm at sea to drive a hero's ship off its course. In the Greek myths, a god or goddess could be a powerful ally, or a terrible foe.

Today, we know the real reasons why storms come up at
sea and why lightning flashes. But we still read Greek myths
because they let us catch a glimpse of a great people of long
ago who did much to shape what we have become. And, of
course, because they are such good stories.

About the Names of Greek and Roman Gods

After the Greeks, another great people rose to power. These people, the Romans, lived in the land now called Italy. Building on the accomplishments of Greece, the ancient Romans made important advancements in law and government. Ancient Rome gave the world heroes, both real and legendary, who still capture our imaginations.

The Romans borrowed many ideas and customs from the Greeks, including their religion. The Romans worshiped the same gods as the Greeks, but called them by different names, as shown in the following table. When you read myths in this and other books, you will sometimes see the Greek names, and sometimes the Roman.

Greek name	Roman name	
Zeus	Jupiter	king of the gods
Hera	Juno	wife of Zeus, queen of the gods
Athena	Minerva	goddess of wisdom
Aphrodite	Venus	goddess of love and beauty
Eros	Cupid	god of love, son of Aphrodite
Ares	Mars	god of war
Artemis	Diana	goddess of the moon and hunting
Demeter	Ceres	goddess of corn and growing things
Hephaestus	Vulcan	god of fire and the forge
Hermes	Mercury	the messenger god
Persephone	Proserpina	daughter of Demeter
Phoebus Apollo	Apollo	god of the sun, music, and poetry
Poseidon	Neptune	god of the sea
Hades	Pluto	god of the underworld

THE GOLDEN AGE

AND WHAT CAME AFTER

THE GOLDEN AGE

In times long past, even before Zeus and his family dwelt on Mount Olympus, a family of gods called the Titans ruled over the heavens and earth. There were twelve of them—six brothers and six sisters—and they said that their father was the Sky and their mother the Earth. They had the form and looks of men and women, but they were taller than mountains and more powerful than a thunderstorm.

The Titans ruled the universe for ages upon ages. The name of the youngest of these Titans was Cronus; and yet he was so very old that men sometimes called him Father Time, for he seemed to have existed as long as time itself.

While Cronus ruled over all, there was a time, men say, when the woods and meadows were always full of blossoms, and the music of singing birds was heard every day and every hour. It was springtime and summer and autumn all at once: apples and figs and oranges always hung ripe from the trees, and there were purple grapes on the vines, and melons and berries of every kind, which the people had but to pick and eat.

This was a Golden Age, a time of peace and plenty. Of course, no one had to do any kind of work in that happy time. There was no such thing as sickness or sorrow or old age. Men and women lived for hundreds and hundreds of years and never became gray or wrinkled but were always handsome and young. They had no need of houses, for there were no cold days nor storms nor anything to make them afraid.

Nobody was poor, for everybody had the same precious things: the sunlight, the pure air, the wholesome water of the springs, the grass for a carpet, the blue sky for a roof, the fruits and flowers of the woods and meadows. No one was richer than another, and there was no money, nor any locks or bolts, for everybody was everybody's friend, and no man wanted to get more of anything than his neighbors had.

During this Golden Age, all the gods and men obeyed the will of Cronus, for indeed, there was no one strong enough to oppose him. And Cronus made sure that no new god should challenge his rule: whenever his wife, Rhea, gave birth to a child, Cronus took the newborn god and swallowed it.

Rhea was determined to find a way to save her children. Thus, when she gave birth to her sixth child, she tricked Cronus into swallowing a stone wrapped in baby clothes. In the meantime, the child, Zeus, was taken to a secret cave, where he fed on ambrosia and nectar, the food and drink of the gods, and quickly grew tall and strong.

As he grew, Zeus began to plot how he might wage war against his father. Through a clever trick, Cronus was persuaded to swallow an herb that he thought would increase his power. Instead, it caused him to vomit up the five children he had swallowed.

Now Zeus had the aid of his brothers and sisters. Together they vowed that they would drive the Titans from the earth.

There followed a long and terrible war. Zeus had many mighty helpers. A company of one-eyed monsters called Cyclopes were kept busy all the time, forging thunderbolts in

wholesome: bringing or supporting good health
forging: forming by heating and hammering

the fire of burning mountains. Three other monsters, each with a hundred hands, were called in to throw rocks and trees against the stronghold of the Titans, and Zeus himself hurled his sharp lightning darts so thick and fast that the woods were set on fire and the water in the rivers boiled with the heat.

Cronos and the other Titans could not hold out against such foes as these, and in time they had to give up and beg for peace. Zeus commanded that they be bound in unbreakable chains and thrown into a prison in the underworld, where the hundred-handed monsters were sent to keep guard over them forever.

Then men, too, began to grow quarrelsome and dissatisfied with their lot. Some wanted to be rich and own all the good things in the world. Some wanted to be kings and rule over the others. Some who were strong wanted to make slaves of those who were weak. Some broke down the fruit trees in the woods, lest others should eat of the fruit.

quarrelsome: likely to fight and argue
lest: for fear that

At last, instead of everybody being everybody's friend, everybody was everybody's foe. Instead of peace, there was war; instead of plenty, there was starvation; instead of innocence, there was crime; and instead of happiness, there was misery.

And that was how Zeus made himself the mighty king of the gods, and how the Golden Age came to an end.

---

foe: enemy

THE STORY OF PROMETHEUS

I. HOW FIRE WAS BROUGHT TO MAN

In these old, old times, there were some among the Titans who were not imprisoned in the underworld. Among these were two brothers, Prometheus and Epimetheus. Let us first hear the story of the wise Prometheus.

Prometheus, whose name means "Forethought," was always thinking of the future and preparing for what might happen tomorrow, next week, next year, and a hundred years to come. Indeed, because he had foreseen the victory of Zeus over Cronus, he had fought on the side of Zeus against the Titans.

Prometheus did not care to live among the clouds on the mountaintop with Zeus and his company. He was too busy for that. While the gods and goddesses were spending their time in idleness, drinking nectar and eating ambrosia, he was intent upon plans for making the world wiser and better than it had ever been before.

So he went among men to live with them and help them, for his heart was filled with sadness when he found that they were no longer happy as they had been during the Golden Age. They were the most miserable of all living creatures, hunted by wild beasts and by one another. They were poor and wretched, living in caves and holes in the earth, dying of starvation and shivering with cold, because there was no fire.

---

idleness: laziness; doing no work nor anything useful
intent upon: focused upon some goal
wretched: miserable

"If only they had fire," said Prometheus to himself, "they could at least warm themselves and cook their food. And after a while, they could learn to make tools and build themselves houses. Without fire, they are worse off than the beasts."

Then he went boldly to Zeus and begged him to give fire to men, so that they might have at least a little comfort in the cold and darkness.

But Zeus replied, "I will not give them even a spark. No, indeed! Why, if men had fire they might become strong and wise like ourselves, and after a while, they would drive us out of our kingdom. Let them shiver with cold and live like the beasts. It is best for them to be poor and ignorant, so that we Mighty Ones may thrive and be happy."

Prometheus made no answer. He had set his heart on helping mankind, and he would not give up. He turned away, and left Zeus and his mighty company forever.

As he was walking by the shore of the sea he found a reed growing. When he had broken it off, he saw that its hollow center was filled with a dry, soft substance that would burn slowly and keep burning a long time. He took the long stalk in his hands and started with it toward the dwelling of the sun far to the east.

"Mankind shall have fire in spite of the tyrant who sits on the mountaintop," he said.

He reached the place of the sun in the early morning just as the glowing, golden orb was rising from the earth and beginning his daily journey through the sky. He touched the

orb: spherical (ball-shaped) object

end of the long reed to the flames, and it caught on fire, burning slowly. Then he turned and hastened back to his own land, carrying with him the precious spark hidden in the plant.

He called some of the shivering men from their caves and built a fire for them, and showed them how to warm themselves by it and how to build other fires from the coals. Soon there was a cheerful blaze in every rude home in the land, and men and women gathered round it and were warm and happy, and thankful to Prometheus for the wonderful gift he had brought to them from the sun.

It was not long until they learned to cook their food and so to eat like men instead of like beasts. They began at once to leave off their wild and savage habits, and instead of lurking in the dark places of the world they came out into the open air and the bright sunlight.

In time, Prometheus taught them a thousand more ways to improve their lives. He showed them how to build houses of wood and stone, and how to tame the sheep and cattle and make them useful, and how to plant and sow and reap, and how to protect themselves from the storms of winter and the beasts of the woods. Then he showed them how to dig in the earth for copper and iron, and how to melt the ore, and how to hammer it into shape and fashion from it the tools and weapons they needed in peace and war.

And when he saw how happy the world was becoming, he cried out, "A new Golden Age shall come, brighter and better by far than the old!"

---

rude: roughly made
lurking: hiding
sow: to plant seeds
reap: to gather or harvest a crop (such as grain)

II. The Wrath of Zeus

Things might have gone on very happily indeed, had it not been for Zeus. One day, when he chanced to look down upon the earth, he saw the fires burning, and the people living in houses, and the flocks feeding on the hills and the grain ripening in the fields. This made him very angry.

"Who has done all this?" he thundered.

And someone answered, "Prometheus!"

"What! That young Titan?" he cried. "Well, I will punish him in a way that will make him wish I had imprisoned him with his kinsfolk."

He commanded two of his servants, whose names were Strength and Force, to seize Prometheus and carry him to the topmost peak of the Caucasus Mountains. Then he sent Hephaestus, the blacksmith of the gods, to bind Prometheus with iron chains and fetter him to the rocks so that he could not move hand or foot.

Hephaestus did not like to do this, for he was a friend of Prometheus. Yet he did not dare to disobey. So the great friend of men, who had given them fire and lifted them out of their wretchedness and showed them how to live, was chained to a mountain peak. There he hung, with the storm winds whistling always around him and the pitiless hail beating in his face, and fierce eagles shrieking in his ears and tearing his body with their cruel claws. Yet he bore all his sufferings without a groan, and never would he beg for mercy or say that he was sorry for what he had done.

Ages passed, and Prometheus remained chained on the mountaintop. Oftentimes men looked up to him with pitying

---

kinsfolk: relatives
fetter: to chain or bind

eyes, and cried out against the tyrant who placed him there. But none could free him from his terrible bondage.

Then, at last, a great hero came, and in spite of Zeus's dread thunderbolts and fearful storms of snow and sleet,

bondage: imprisonment; captivity
dread: causing great fear

he climbed the rugged mountain peak and slew the fierce eagles that had so long tormented the helpless prisoner on those craggy heights. Then, with a mighty blow, he broke Prometheus's fetters, and set free the bold friend of all mankind.

"I knew you would come," said Prometheus to the young hero. "But, please, tell me your name so I may thank you properly."

And the brave young man replied, "I am called Hercules."

---

slew: killed
tormented: caused great pain to
craggy: jagged; steep, rough, and rocky

THE STORY OF PANDORA

I. PANDORA, THE ALL-GIFTED

When Prometheus gave fire to man, Zeus's wrath was so great that not only did he punish Prometheus, he also wished to punish all mankind.

"Let those puny men keep their fire," he raged. "I will make them ten times more miserable than they were before they had it."

So he ordered his blacksmith Hephaestus, whose forge was in the crater of a burning mountain, to take a lump of clay that he gave him, and mold it into the form of a woman. Hephaestus did as he was bidden, and when he had finished the image, he carried it up to Zeus, who was sitting among the clouds with all the gods and goddesses around him. It was nothing but a mere lifeless body, but the great blacksmith had given it a form more perfect than that of any statue that has ever been made.

"Come now," said Zeus, "let us all give our best gifts to the woman," and he began by giving her life.

Then the others came in their turn, each with a gift for the marvelous creature. One gave her beauty, and another a pleasant voice, and another good manners, and another a kind heart, and another skill in many arts, and lastly, someone gave her curiosity. And they called her Pandora, which means "the all-gifted," because she had received gifts from them all.

---

puny: small and weak
bidden: commanded

Pandora was so beautiful and so wondrously gifted that no one could help but love her. After the dwellers on Mount Olympus had admired her for a time, they had Hermes, the swift-footed messenger of the gods, lead her down the mountainside to the place where the brother of Prometheus lived.

This brother was named Epimetheus, which means Afterthought. And as much as Prometheus planned for the future, Epimetheus thought of the past. He was always busy thinking of yesterday, or last year, or a hundred years ago, and had no care at all for what might come to pass in the days or months or years ahead.

Prometheus had often warned his brother to beware of any gift that Zeus might send, for he knew that the mighty tyrant could not be trusted. But when Hermes came down from the mountaintop with Pandora and said to him, "Epimetheus, Zeus favors you! Here is a beautiful woman, whom he has sent to be your wife," Epimetheus forgot all warnings. He thought of nothing but the lovely lady, and took her home to be his wife.

II. The Golden Casket

Pandora was very happy in her new home. She had brought with her a golden casket that Zeus had given her.

"Inside are many precious things," Zeus had said. "Keep them well."

---

casket: a small box for storing valuable objects

But wise Athena had added, "It is enough to be trusted with keeping the casket. Never, never open it, nor try to see what is inside."

But each time Pandora looked at the casket, her curiosity grew about what might lie within it.

"They must be jewels," she said to herself, and then she thought of how they would add to her beauty if only she could wear them. "Why did Zeus give them to me if I should never use them, nor so much as look at them?" she asked.

The more she thought about the golden casket, the more she longed to see what was in it. Finally, she took it down from its shelf, felt around the lid, and tried to peer inside without opening it.

"Why should I care for what Athena told me?" she said at last. "She is not beautiful, and jewels would be of no use to her. What could it hurt if I just peeped inside and closed the lid again? Athena will never know. No one will ever know."

So she opened the lid a very little. All at once, there was a whirring, rustling sound, and before she could shut the lid, out flew ten thousand strange creatures with death-like faces and gaunt and dreadful forms, shrieking and wailing, and reaching out for her with cold, bony hands. They were diseases, troubles, and cares; for up until that time, mankind had not had any sickness, nor felt any hurt, nor worried about what the next day might bring.

The terrible creatures chased each other around the room, and then flew away out the window to find dwelling places wherever there were homes of men. They entered every house without anyone seeing them, crept into the hearts of men and women and children, and put an end to all their joy. And every day since, they have been flitting and creeping,

gaunt: extremely thin and bony

unseen and unheard, over all the land, bringing pain and sorrow and sickness into every household.

This was how Zeus sought to make mankind even more miserable than they had been before Prometheus had befriended them.

III. THE LAST VOICE

When Pandora slammed shut the lid of the casket, then for the first time in her life she knew misery. A thousand troubles and terrors ran through her head.

"What will become of me?" she wondered, tears welling up in her eyes. "And what will become of mankind?"

Suddenly, there came a gentle tap on the inside of the casket's lid.

"Who is that?" asked Pandora.

"Lift the lid, and you shall see," said a voice from within the casket.

"No," cried Pandora. "I have had enough of lifting the lid. You are inside the box, and there you will stay. Ten thousand of your brothers and sisters are bringing misery to the world. Do not think that I would be so foolish as to let you out to join them!"

"I am not like those evil creatures," said the voice. "And do not despair, for matters are not as terrible as they seem. Lift the lid, and I will show you."

With each word the voice spoke, Pandora felt her heart growing lighter. She flung open the lid of the box, and out flew a beautiful creature with a sweet face, whose golden glow lit up even the darkest corners of the room.

"I am Hope," said the beautiful creature, kissing Pandora on the forehead. "I will make amends for that swarm of troubles. Do not fear! We will do well in spite of them all."

Pandora felt her spirits rise. "Will you stay here with me forever?" she asked.

"I will stay as long as you need me," Hope replied. "There will come times when you think I have left the earth entirely, but again and again, in times of trouble, you will see the glimmer of my wings. Even Zeus's wrath cannot destroy me or dim my glow. Never fear, child, for good things await you."

Then she took Pandora by the hand, and they went out together to bring joy and promise back into the world.

---

despair: to lose all hope
make amends: to make up for some loss, injury, or mistake

QUESTS AND ADVENTURES

THE THINGS THAT HAVEN'T BEEN DONE BEFORE

by Edgar Guest

The things that haven't been done before,
    Those are the things to try;
Columbus dreamed of an unknown shore
    At the rim of the far-flung sky,
And his heart was bold and his faith was strong
    As he ventured in dangers new,
And he paid no heed to the jeering throng
    Or the fears of the doubting crew.

The many will follow the beaten track
    With guideposts on the way.
They live and have lived for ages back
    With a chart for every day.
Someone has told them it's safe to go
    On the road he has traveled o'er,
And all that they ever strive to know
    Are the things that were known before.

---

ventured: undertook or proceeded in something risky
heed: attention
jeering: taunting; mocking
throng: crowd
o'er: poetic form of the word "over"

A few strike out, without map or chart,
    Where never a man has been,
From the beaten paths they draw apart
    To see what no man has seen.
There are deeds they hunger alone to do;
    Though battered and bruised and sore,
They blaze the path for the many, who
    Do nothing not done before.

The things that haven't been done before
    Are the tasks worthwhile today;
Are you one of the flock that follows, or
    Are you one that shall lead the way?
Are you one of the timid souls that quail
    At the jeers of a doubting crew,
Or dare you, whatever you win or fail,
    Strike out for a goal that's new?

---

timid: fearful
quail: act cowardly or afraid

PERSEUS AND THE QUEST FOR MEDUSA'S HEAD

I: THE KING'S CRUEL CHALLENGE

Long ago in Greece, there lived a proud and daring young man named Perseus. His bold ways earned him the love of his fellows but also the anger of the king. The king of the land was both jealous and cruel, and soon he could think of nothing but how to shame Perseus and be rid of him forever.

One day, the king called all the noble young men of his country together and told them that he was soon to marry a queen from beyond the sea. He asked each of them to bring him a present to be given to the bride's father, for in those times it was the custom that when any man was to be married, he must offer costly gifts to the father of the bride.

"What kind of presents do you want?" said the young men.

"Horses," answered the king, for he knew that Perseus himself had no horses to give.

Perseus was vexed by the king's request, which he knew was meant to shame him. Impulsively he cried out, "Horses— is that all you ask? Why don't you ask for something worth having? Why don't you ask for Medusa's head?"

Upon hearing this, the king smiled triumphantly. "Then Medusa's head it shall be!" he said. "These young men may

---

vexed: annoyed; distressed
impulsively: without thinking ahead
triumphantly: in the manner of celebrating some victory

give me horses, but you, Perseus, must bring me the head
of Medusa."

"And so I will," said Perseus grimly, and he went away in
anger, while his young friends laughed at him because of his
foolish words.

What was this Medusa's head which Perseus had so
rashly promised to bring?

Far, far away, on the very edge of the world, said the
Greeks, there lived three strange monsters, sisters called
Gorgons. They had the bodies and faces of women, but they
had wings of gold, terrible claws of brass, and hair that was
full of living serpents. They were so awful to look upon that
any man who saw their faces was turned to stone. Two of
these monsters had charmed lives, and no weapon could
ever do them harm, but the third, whose name was Medusa,
might be killed, if indeed anyone could find her and give her
the fatal stroke.

grimly: with stern determination
rashly: thoughtlessly; hastily

When Perseus went away from the king's palace, he began to feel sorry that he had spoken so rashly. He walked down to the sea, wondering, "How will I ever make good my promise and meet the king's challenge? I do not know which way to go to find the Gorgons, and I have no weapon with which to slay the terrible Medusa. Still, I will never show my face to the king again, unless I bring the monster's head with me."

As Perseus thought, the sun went down and the moon arose and a soft wind came blowing from the west. Then, all at once, a man and a woman stood before him. Both were tall and noble. The man looked like a prince. There were wings on his cap and sandals, and he carried a winged staff, around which two golden serpents were twined.

"What is the matter, Perseus?" he asked, and Perseus told him how the king had treated him, and about the rash words he had spoken.

The lady replied, "Do not fear. Go out boldly in quest of the Gorgons, and we will help you obtain Medusa's terrible head." And as she spoke, Perseus noticed that although she was not beautiful, she had most wonderful gray eyes, a stern but lovable face, and a queenly form.

"But I have no horses and no ship. How will I get there?" said Perseus.

"You shall don my winged sandals," said the strange prince, "and they will bear you over sea and land."

"But how will I know where to go?" asked Perseus.

"I will tell you," said the queenly lady. "You must go first to the three Gray Sisters, who live beyond the frozen sea in the far, far north. They alone know where to find the maidens who guard the golden apples of the Western Land. The maidens will give you what you need to kill Medusa, and they will tell you how to reach the edge of the world where lies the home of the Gorgons."

Then the man took off his winged sandals, and put them on Perseus's feet, and the queenly lady whispered, "Be off at once, Perseus. Be bold and true, and fear nothing."

And Perseus knew that she was none other than Athena, the queen of the air, and that her companion was Hermes, the prince of the summer clouds. But before he could thank them for their kindness, they vanished in the dusky twilight.

II: The Gray Sisters

Perseus strapped on Hermes's winged sandals and leaped into the air. Swifter than an eagle, he flew through the sky, as the sandals carried him north over the sea, over cities and towns, over ranges of snowy mountains, and at last to the sea of ice. On he flew, among toppling icebergs, over frozen billows, and through air that the sun never warmed, until at last he came to the mouth of the cavern where the three Gray Sisters lived.

These three creatures were so old that they had forgotten their own age, and nobody could count how many years they had lived. Their long hair had been gray since they were born, and they had among them only a single eye and a single tooth, which they passed back and forth. Perseus heard them mumbling and crooning in their dreary home, and he listened.

"We know a secret which even the Great Folk who live on the mountaintop can never learn, don't we, sisters?" said one.

billows: waves
crooning: speaking softly and gently
dreary: cheerless; gloomy

"Ha ha! That we do, that we do!" chattered the others. "We will never tell, never tell our secret. Not to man, not even to the Great Folk on the mountain!"

"Oh, we are clever! Give me the tooth, sister, that I may feel young and handsome again, too," said the one nearest to Perseus.

"And give me the eye that I may look out and see what is going on in the busy world," said the sister who sat next to her.

"Yes, yes," mumbled the third. And she took the tooth and the eye and reached them blindly toward the others.

Then, quick as thought, Perseus leaped forward and snatched both of the precious things from her hand.

"Where is the tooth? Where is the eye?" screamed the two, reaching out their long arms and groping here and there. "Have you dropped them, sister? Have you lost them?"

"I have your tooth and your eye," said Perseus, "and I will not give them back until you tell me your secret. Where are the maidens who keep the golden apples of the Western Land? Tell me how to find them!"

"Ah, sisters, we must tell him," whined one.

"Yes, we must tell him," moaned the others. "We must part with the secret to save our tooth and our eye."

So they told him how to reach the Western Land, and what road to follow to find the maidens who kept the golden apples. When they had made everything plain to him, Perseus gave them back their eye and tooth.

"Ha!" they laughed, "now the golden days of youth have come again!" And from that day to this, no man has ever seen the three Gray Sisters, nor does anyone know what became of them. The winds still whistle through their

groping: searching blindly

cheerless cave, the cold waves murmur on the shore of the wintry sea, and the ice mountains topple and crash, but no sound of living creature has since been heard in all that desolate land.

III. The Maidens of the Western Land

Perseus left the cave of the Gray Sisters and leaped into the air. The winged sandals bore him south with the speed of the wind. Very soon he left the frozen sea behind him and came to a sunny land with tall forests, green meadows and valleys, and at last a pleasant garden teeming with all kinds of flowers and fruits.

The young man knew that this was the famous Western Land, for the Gray Sisters had told him what he should see there. He walked among the trees until he came to the center of the garden. There he came upon the three maidens singing and dancing around a tree heavy with golden apples. The wonderful tree with its precious fruit belonged to Hera, queen of earth and sky, and it was the maidens' duty to care for it and see that no one touched the golden apples.

Perseus stopped and listened to their song:

> We sing of the old, we sing of the new —
> Our joys are many, our sorrows are few;
> Singing, dancing,
> All hearts entrancing,
> We wait to welcome the good and the true.

---

desolate: bare; lifeless
teeming: abounding; filled to overflowing

The daylight is waning, the evening is here,
The sun will soon set, the stars will appear.
Singing, dancing,
All hearts entrancing,
We wait for the dawn of a glad new year.

The tree shall wither, the apples shall fall,
Sorrow shall come, and death shall call,
Alarming, grieving,
All hearts deceiving,
But hope shall abide to comfort us all.

Soon the tale shall be told, the song shall be sung,
The bow shall be broken, the harp unstrung,
Alarming, grieving,
All hearts deceiving,
Till every joy to the winds shall be flung.

But a new tree shall spring from the roots of the old,
And many a blossom its leaves shall unfold,
Cheering, gladdening,
With joy maddening,
For its boughs shall be laden with apples of gold.

Then Perseus went forward and spoke to the maidens. They stopped singing, and stood still as if in alarm. But when they saw the winged sandals on his feet, they ran to him, and welcomed him to the Western Land and to their garden.

"We knew that you were coming," they said, "for the winds told us. But why have you come?"

"I am on a quest to slay the monster Medusa," he said. "I have come to ask your help. Tell me, fair maidens, where I

---

laden: heavily filled

may find the monster's lair, and with what weapon I might slay it."

"We will do better than tell you," laughed the maidens, and the first came forward and buckled to Perseus's side a sword made of adamant. The second gave him a shield polished as brightly as a mirror. The third gave him a pouch that she hung by a long strap over his shoulder.

"With these three things, you will be able to slay the monster," said the maidens. "But here is a fourth, for without it, your quest will be in vain." And they gave him the Cap of Darkness, and when they had put it upon his head, not a creature on the earth or in the sky, not even the maidens themselves, could see him.

Then they told him where he would find the Gorgons, and what he should do to obtain the terrible head and escape alive. They wished him good luck, and bade him hasten to do the dangerous deed. So Perseus donned the Cap of Darkness and sped away and away toward the edge of the earth, while the three maidens went back to their tree to sing and to dance and to guard the golden apples until the old world should become young again.

IV. The Dreadful Gorgons

With the keen-edged sword at his side and the bright shield upon his arm, Perseus flew bravely in search of the dreadful Gorgons. Because he also wore the Cap of Darkness, you could no more have seen him than you can see the wind. He flew so swiftly that it was not long until he had crossed the

---

adamant: a stone, like a diamond, once believed to be unbreakable
in vain: useless
hasten: to hurry

ocean and come to the sunless land where the lair of the Gorgons lay.

He heard a sound as of someone breathing heavily, and he looked around to see where it came from. Among the foul weeds growing close to the bank of a muddy river, something glittered in the pale light. He flew a little nearer, but he did not dare to look straight forward, lest he should all at once meet the gaze of a Gorgon and be turned to stone. So he flew backwards, and used the shining shield like a mirror to see the objects behind him.

And what a dreadful sight it was! Half hidden among the weeds lay the three monsters, fast asleep, with their golden wings folded about them. Their brazen claws were stretched out as though ready to seize their prey, and their heads and shoulders were covered with sleeping snakes. The two largest of the Gorgons lay with their heads tucked under their wings, as birds hide their heads when they go to sleep. But the third, which lay between them, slept with her face turned up toward the sky, and Perseus knew that she was Medusa.

Very stealthily he went nearer and nearer, always with his back toward the monsters and always looking into his bright shield to see where to go. Then he drew his sword, and dashing quickly downward, struck a blow so sure and swift that the head of Medusa was cut from her shoulders. Without looking, he thrust the terrible head into his pouch and leaped again into the air, flying away with the speed of the wind.

Then the two older Gorgons awoke and rose with dreadful screams, and spread their great wings and dashed after him. They could not see him, for the Cap of Darkness hid him even from their eyes. But they scented the blood of

brazen: made of brass, or having the color of polished brass

the head that he carried in his pouch, and like hounds in the chase, they followed him, sniffing the air.

As he flew through the clouds, he could hear their dreadful cries and the clatter of their golden wings and the snapping of their horrible jaws. But Hermes's winged sandals were faster than any monster's wings. In a little while, the cries of the Gorgons were heard no more, and Perseus flew on alone.

V. The Great Sea Beast

Again Perseus crossed the great ocean and flew east until he came to a country where there were palm trees and pyramids and a great river flowing from the south. Here, as he looked down, a strange sight met his eyes. He saw a beautiful girl chained to a rock by the seashore, and far away, a huge sea beast swimming toward her to devour her. Without the least hesitation, he flew down and took off the Cap of Darkness.

"Oh, help me!" cried the girl when she saw the young hero, and she reached out her arms toward him.

Perseus drew his sword and cut the chain that held her, and then lifted her high upon the rock. But by this time, the sea monster was close at hand. It lashed the water with its tail and opened its wide jaws as though it would swallow not only Perseus and the young girl, but even the rock on which they were standing.

"Close your eyes!" Perseus cried to the girl. Then he swiftly pulled the head of Medusa from his pouch and held it up. The moment the monster saw the dreadful face, it stopped short and was turned to stone. And men say that the stone beast may be seen in that same spot to this day.

---

devour: to eat greedily
lashed: whipped

Then Perseus slipped the Gorgon's head back into the pouch, turned to the girl, and asked, "What is your name? And why are you here?"

"My name is Andromeda," the girl replied. "I am the daughter of the king of this land. My mother, the queen, was very beautiful and very proud of her beauty. Every day she came down to the seashore to look at her face in the water, and she boasted that not even the nymphs who live in the sea were as beautiful as she. When the sea nymphs heard this, they were very angry and asked Poseidon, the king of the sea, to punish my mother for her pride. So Poseidon sent the sea monster to crush our ships and kill the cattle along the shore and break down all the fishermen's huts.

"At last, my father was so distressed that he sent to Delphi to ask the oracle what he should do. And the oracle said that there was only one way to save the kingdom—that they must give me to the sea monster to be devoured.

"For a long time, my mother and father refused to do as the oracle said. But day after day, the monster laid waste to our land, and threatened to destroy not only the farms, but the towns as well. So I was chained to this rock and left to perish in the jaws of that awful beast."

As Andromeda told her story, the king and the queen, along with a great company of people, came down the shore, weeping and tearing their hair, for they were sure that by this time the monster had devoured the lovely princess. But when they saw her alive and well, and learned that she had been saved by the brave young man who stood beside her, their great grief turned to even greater joy.

---

oracle: in mythology, a being who was believed to have knowledge from the gods

"I will give you anything you wish as a reward for saving my daughter," cried the king. "Anything."

Perseus reached out his hand to the lovely girl and said, "What I wish most is for Andromeda to be my wife."

The king laughed heartily at Perseus's boldness and happily agreed. So Perseus and Andromeda were married, and there was a great feast in the king's palace, and everybody was merry and glad.

VI. The Journey's End

The two young people lived happily for some time in the land of palms and pyramids, but Perseus had not forgotten the challenge of the king who had sent him in quest of Medusa's head. One fine summer day, he and Andromeda sailed in a beautiful ship to his own home, for the winged sandals could not carry both him and his bride through the air.

When they arrived, Perseus went straight to the king, held up the pouch, and cried, "I promised to bring you Medusa's head, and here it is!"

"Nonsense!" scoffed the king. "A boy like you could no more kill Medusa than a wild boar. Take your pig's head, boy, and go play somewhere else." And all the court laughed.

But Perseus's eyes flashed fire and he asked, "Wouldn't you like to see it? Or are you afraid of this pig's head?"

"Show us," growled the king, his brows knit together in anger.

To the lords and ladies of the court, Perseus called out, "I charge you, if you value your lives, turn away, for this sight

charge: to command

is for the king's eyes only." And he spoke so sternly that no one dared to ignore his warning.

Then with one swift motion, just as the king was drawing his sword to strike, Perseus lifted the head of terror from the pouch. The king saw it and was turned into stone, just as he stood, with his sword uplifted and his face twisted with anger.

But the people of the land were glad when they learned what had happened, for no one loved the cruel king. They were glad, too, because Perseus had come home again and had brought with him his lovely wife, Andromeda. So, after the people had talked the matter over among themselves, they went to Perseus and asked him to be their king.

"I thank you," he said, "and I will gladly rule over you, but for one day only. Then I will give the kingdom to another, for other adventures await me upon other shores."

For that one day, he ruled the land, but on the morrow, he gave the kingdom to a fisherman he had known from his youth, whose wisdom all admired and whose judgment everyone trusted. Then he went on board his ship with Andromeda, and sailed away across the sea.

on the morrow: the next day

Atalanta, the Fleet-Footed Huntress

I. The Bear on the Mountain

In a sunny land in Greece called Arcadia, there lived a king and a queen who had no children. They wanted very much to have a son who might live to rule over Arcadia when the king was dead. And after many years, a child was born to them, but it was a little girl.

"What is a girl good for?" raged the king. "She can never do anything but sing and spin. If the child had been a boy, he might have learned to do many things—to ride, to hunt, and to fight in the wars, and by and by, he would rule as king of Arcadia. But this girl can never be a king."

Then in his wild rage he called to one of his men and bade him take the babe out to a mountain where there was nothing but rocks and thick woods and leave it there. The man carried the child far up the mountainside and laid it down on a bed of moss in the shadow of a great rock. The child stretched out its baby hands toward him and smiled, but he turned away and left it there, for he did not dare to disobey the king.

For a whole night and a whole day the babe lay on its bed of moss, wailing for its mother, but only the birds among the trees heard its pitiful cries. At last it grew so weak for want of

---

bade: ordered
pitiful: sad; deserving compassion

food that it could only moan and move its head a little from side to side.

Just before dark on the second evening, a she-bear came strolling down the mountainside from her den. She was looking for her cubs, for some hunters had stolen them that very day while she was away from home, and they were nowhere to be found.

As the stars came out, the she-bear heard the babe's moans and saw it lying helpless on its bed of moss. She looked at it kindly, licked its face with her warm tongue, and then lay down beside it, just as she would have done with her own little cubs. The babe was too young to feel afraid, and it cuddled close to the old bear and felt that it had found a friend. After a while it fell asleep, but the bear guarded it until morning and then went down the mountainside to look for food.

In the evening, the bear came again and carried the child to her own den under the shelter of a rock where vines and wild flowers grew, and every day after that she came and gave the child food and played with it. Soon, all the bears on the mountain learned about the wonderful cub and came to see it, and not one of them tried to harm it.

The little girl grew quickly and became strong. After a while, she could walk and run among the trees and rocks and brambles on the round top of the mountain; but her bear mother would not allow her to wander far from the den beneath the rock where the vines and the wild flowers grew.

One day, some hunters came up the mountain to look for game. One of them pulled aside the vines that grew in front of the old bear's home. He was surprised to see the beautiful child lying on the grass and playing with the flowers she had gathered. But at sight of him, she leaped to her feet and bounded away like a frightened deer. She led the hunters on a fine chase among the trees and rocks, but there were a dozen of them and by circling her they managed at last to catch her.

The child struggled and fought as hard as she knew how, but it was no use. The hunters carried her down the mountain, and took her to the house where they lived on the other side of the forest. At first she cried all the time, for she sadly missed the bear that had been a mother to her for so long. But the hunters were very kind and treated her like their daughter. And so, slowly, she also came to like her new home.

The hunters named the girl Atalanta. When she grew older, they made her a bow and arrows and taught her how to shoot, and they gave her a light spear and showed her how to carry it and how to hurl it at game or at an enemy. They took her with them when they went hunting, and there was nothing in the world that pleased her so much as roaming through the woods and running after the deer and other wild animals. Her feet became very swift, so that she could run faster than any of the men. Her arms were so strong and her eyes so sharp that with her arrow or her spear she never missed the mark. And she grew up to be very tall and graceful, and was known throughout all Arcadia as Atalanta, the fleet-footed huntress.

II. The Wild Boar of Calydon

Not very far from the land of Arcadia there was a little city named Calydon. It lay in the midst of rich wheat fields and fruitful vineyards, but beyond the vineyards was a deep, dense forest where many wild beasts lived. One day, the largest and fiercest wild boar that anybody had ever seen came rushing out of the forest. It had two long tusks which stuck far out of its mouth on either side and were as sharp as knives, and the stiff bristles on its back were as long as knitting needles.

The wild boar raced towards Calydon, champing its teeth and foaming at the mouth. It rushed into the wheat fields and tore up all the grain, it charged into the vineyard and broke down all the vines, it rooted up all the trees in the orchards, and when there was nothing else to do, it hurtled into the pastures among the hills and killed the sheep that were feeding there.

The beast was so fierce and so swift that everyone fled before it. Its thick skin was proof against arrows and against such spears as the people of Calydon had, and many brave warriors who tried to attack the boar died at the edge of its terrible razor tusks. For weeks, it ran wild about the countryside, and the only safe place for anybody was inside the city walls.

At last, when it had laid waste to much of the country, the boar went back into the edge of the forest. But the people were so much afraid of it that they lived in constant dread that the beast should come again and tear down the gates of the city.

dense: thick
champing: chewing loudly and impatiently; gnashing
hurtled: rushed forcefully

So the king of Calydon sent messengers into all the countries nearby, asking the bravest men and the most skillful hunters to come at a certain time and help him hunt and kill the great wild boar. When the day came, there was a wonderful gathering of men at Calydon. The greatest heroes in the world were there. Everyone was fully armed, and all expected to have fine sport hunting the terrible beast. With the warriors from the south came Atalanta, armed with bow and arrows and a long hunting spear.

"My daughters are having a game of ball in the garden," said the king to the huntress. "Would you like to put away your arrows and your spear and go play with them?"

Atalanta shook her head and lifted her chin in disdain.

"Perhaps you would rather stay with the queen, and look at the women spin and weave," said the king.

"No," answered Atalanta. "I am going with the warriors to hunt the wild boar in the forest."

The men gasped. They had never heard of such a thing as a girl going out with heroes to hunt wild boars.

"If she goes, then I will not," muttered one.

"Nor will I," said another, a little more loudly. "Why, the whole world would laugh at us, and we should never hear the end of it."

"Nor will I," exclaimed a third. "The hunt is for heroes, not for girls."

Many of the men guffawed and hooted at the young huntress. But Atalanta only grasped her spear more firmly and stood tall and straight in the gateway of the palace.

Just then, the youngest prince of Calydon came forward. His name was Meleager.

---

disdain: scorn; contempt
guffawed: laughed loudly

"What's this?" he cried. "Who says that Atalanta shall not go to the hunt? Why, I believe you are afraid that she'll be braver than you. Fine heroes you are! Let all such cowards go home at once."

All laughter died away in a moment, and not a single man moved. And it was settled then and there that Atalanta would go with the heroes to hunt the wild boar, though some of the men kept muttering and complaining among themselves.

For nine days, the heroes and huntsmen feasted in the halls of the king of Calydon. Early on the tenth, they set out for the forest. Soon they came upon the great beast, which came charging out upon his foes.

The heroes hid behind the trees or climbed up among the branches, for they had not expected to see so terrible a creature. The boar stood in the middle of a glade, pawing the ground with his hooves, and tearing it up with his tusks. White foam rolled from his mouth, his eyes glistened like red fire, and he grunted so fiercely that the woods and hills echoed with fearful sounds.

One of the bravest of the men threw his spear, but that only made the beast fiercer than ever. He charged the warrior, caught him before he could scramble into a tree, and tore him to pieces in a mad fury. Another man leapt out from his hiding place and was also killed. Then one of the oldest and noblest of the heroes launched his spear with a mighty heave, but it only grazed the boar's tough skin and glanced away. The boar was getting the best of the fight.

Softly, Atalanta stepped out into the glade. She leveled her spear, and threw it with all her might. The boar squealed as the sharp point pierced its skin. It ran about in a frenzy,

---

frenzy: wild, frantic activity

heedless of the hunters and their arrows and spears. Then Meleager rushed up and thrust his spear into its heart. The terrible creature thrashed and then rolled over, dead.

The heroes then cut off the boar's skin and offered it to Meleager as a prize, because he had given the boar its death wound.

But Meleager said, "It belongs to Atalanta, because it was she who wounded the boar first." And he gave the skin to her as the prize of honor.

III. ATALANTA'S RACE

After the hunt at Calydon, Atalanta went back to her old home among the mountains of Arcadia. She was still the fleet-footed huntress, and she was never so happy as when in the green woods wandering among the trees or chasing the wild deer. All the world had heard about her, however, and the young heroes in the lands nearest to Arcadia did nothing else but talk about her beauty, grace, swiftness, and courage.

---

heedless: paying no attention to; thoughtless

Of course every one of these young fellows wanted her to become his wife, and she might have been a queen any day if she had only said the word, for the richest king in Greece would have been glad to marry her. But she cared nothing for any of the young men. She preferred the freedom of the green woods to all the luxuries she might have enjoyed in a palace.

But the young men would not take "No!" for an answer. They could not believe that she really meant it, so they kept coming and staying until the woods of Arcadia were full of them, and there was no getting along with them at all.

So when she could think of no other way to get rid of them, Atalanta called them together and said, "You want to marry me, do you? Well, if any one of you would like to run a race with me from this mountain to the riverbank, he may do so. I will be the wife of the one who outruns me."

"Agreed! Agreed!" cried all the young fellows.

"But listen!" she said. "Whoever tries this race must also agree that if I outrun him, he must lose his life."

The men glanced furtively at one another. Many of them drew away from the crowd, melted into the trees, and turned their hurried footsteps towards home.

Those who stayed said, "We agree. But if we are to risk our lives, won't you at least give us a head start?"

"As you wish," she answered. "I will give you a start of a hundred paces. But remember, if I overtake anyone before he reaches the river, he shall lose his life that very day."

Several others now decided that they were not feeling well or that business called them home, so they also left the crowd. But a few who had some practice sprinting across the country

luxuries: unnecessary comforts
furtively: slyly; sneakily

stayed and made up their minds to try their luck. Could a mere girl outrun such fine fellows as they? Nonsense!

And so it happened that a race was run almost every day, and almost every day some poor fellow lost his life, for the swiftest sprinter in all Greece was overtaken by Atalanta long before he could reach the riverbank.

Then one day there came from a distant land a fine young man named Hippomenes. Atalanta liked his kind expression and his courteous manner. She dearly hoped that this young man would not put himself to the test in a race against her.

"You had better not run with me," said Atalanta, "for I am sure to overtake you, and you will lose your life."

"Ah, my good lady, that remains to be seen," replied Hippomenes, with a curious twinkle in his eyes. For before he had come to try his chance, Hippomenes had sought the help of Aphrodite, the queen of love, who lived among the clouds on Mount Olympus. And Hippomenes was so gentle and wise and brave that Aphrodite took pity on him. She gave him three golden apples and told him how he might use them to defeat the fleet-footed huntress in a race.

On the day of the race, Atalanta tried again to persuade Hippomenes not to run, for she also took pity on him.

"I'm sure to overtake you," she said. "Please, don't lose your life needlessly."

"I won't," laughed Hippomenes, and away he sped. But in his pocket, he carried Aphrodite's three golden apples.

Atalanta gave him a good start and then she followed after, as swift as an arrow shot from the bow. Hippomenes was not a very fast runner, and it would not be hard for her to overtake him. She thought that she would let him get almost to the goal, for she really pitied him. But when he

---

courteous: polite; considerate

heard her quick breath behind him, he threw one of the golden apples over his shoulder.

As the apple fell to the ground, Atalanta saw how beautiful it was, and she stopped to pick it up. While she was doing this, Hippomenes gained a good many paces. But in a minute she was as close behind him as ever.

And yet, she really did pity him.

Just then, Hippomenes threw the second apple over his shoulder. It was handsomer and larger than the first, and Atalanta could not bear the thought of allowing someone else to get it. So she stopped to pick it up from where it had fallen among the long grass. It took longer to find it than she had expected, and when she looked up again, Hippomenes was a hundred feet ahead of her. But that was no matter; she could easily overtake him.

And yet, how she did pity the foolish young man!

Hippomenes heard her footsteps thundering just a few paces behind him. He took the third apple and threw it over to one side of the path where the ground sloped toward the river. Atalanta's quick eye saw that it was far more beautiful than either of the others. If it were not picked up at once, it would roll down into the deep water and be lost, and that would never do. She turned aside from her course and ran after it. It was easy enough to retrieve the apple, but while she was doing so, Hippomenes gained upon her again. He was almost to the riverbank. How she strained every muscle now to overtake him!

But after all, she felt that she did not care very much. He was the finest young man that she had ever seen, he had given her three golden apples, and he had risked his life to win her. It would be a great pity if he should have to die.

So she slowed her steps, and let him reach the riverbank first.

After that, Atalanta became Hippomenes's wife. And the young man took the fleet-footed huntress with him to his distant home, and there they lived happily together for many, many years.

THE ADVENTURES OF THESEUS

I. SWORD AND SANDALS

Once, long ago, there lived a tall, ruddy-cheeked lad named Theseus. On the day Theseus turned fifteen years old, he went with his mother to the top of a mountain and looked out with her over the sea.

"Ah, if only your father would come!" she sighed.

"My father?" said Theseus, "Who is my father, and why are you always watching and waiting and wishing that he would come? Tell me about him."

She answered, "My child, do you see the great flat stone lying there under that tree, half buried in the ground, covered with moss and trailing ivy? Do you think you can lift it?"

"I do not know, but I will surely try," said Theseus. And he dug his fingers into the ground beside it, grasped its uneven edges, and tugged and strained until his breath came hard and his arms ached and his body was covered with sweat. Still, the stone would not budge. At last he said, "The task is too hard for me until I have grown stronger. But why do you wish me to lift it?"

"When you are strong enough to lift it," she answered, "I will tell you about your father."

After that, the boy went out every day and practiced running and leaping and throwing and lifting, and every day he rolled some stone out of its place. At first he could move only a little weight, and those who saw him laughed as he

ruddy: healthy red

pulled and puffed and grew red in the face, but never gave up until he had lifted it. And little by little he grew stronger, and his muscles became like iron bands.

On his next birthday, he went again up the mountain with his mother, and again tried to lift the great stone. But it remained fast in its place and was not moved.

"I am not yet strong enough, mother," he said.

"Have patience, my son," she replied.

So Theseus went on with his running and leaping and throwing and lifting. He practiced wrestling also, and tamed the wild horses of the plain, and hunted the lions among the mountains. His strength and swiftness and skill were the wonder of all men, and the land was filled with tales of his deeds.

Yet when Theseus tried again on his seventeenth birthday, he still could not move the great flat stone on the mountainside.

"Have patience, my son," his mother said, but this time there were tears in her eyes.

So Theseus went back again to his exercising, and he learned to wield a sword and a battle-ax, and to throw tremendous weights, and to carry great burdens. And men said that since the days of Hercules there was never such great strength in one body.

Then on the day he turned eighteen, Theseus climbed the mountain yet again with his mother. He stooped and took hold of the stone, and it yielded to his touch. When he had lifted it quite out of the ground, he found underneath it a sword of bronze and sandals of gold, and these he gave to her.

"Tell me now about my father," he said.

---

wield: to handle with skill

She said, "My son, your father is Aegeus, king of Athens. He himself lifted the great stone and laid the sword and sandals beneath it. Strong as he is, at his court also live your fifty cousins, who wish to be king when he dies, so he bade us stay here, far from any harm that they might do you. When you were but a babe, your father, the king, said that when you grew strong enough to lift the great stone, then you must take the sword and sandals and go seek him in Athens."

Then she buckled the sword to his belt and fastened the sandals upon his feet. Theseus's proud eyes flashed with eagerness, and he said, "I am ready, mother, and I will set out for Athens this very day."

Then they walked down the mountain together and told Theseus's grandfather what had happened, and showed him the sword and the sandals. But the old man shook his head sadly and tried to dissuade Theseus from going.

"How can you go to Athens in these lawless times?" he said. "The sea is full of pirates. In fact, no ship from this land has sailed across the sea since your kingly father went home to his people, eighteen years ago."

Then, finding that this only made Theseus the more determined, he said, "If you must go, I will have a new ship built for you, strong and fast, and fifty of the bravest young men in the kingdom shall go with you. Perhaps, with fair winds and fearless hearts, you will escape the pirates and reach Athens in safety."

"Which is the most dangerous way?" asked Theseus. "To sail a ship across the sea or to make the journey on foot along the coast?"

---

dissuade: to advise not to do something

"The sea is full enough of dangers," said his grandfather, "but the land route is riddled with dangers much greater. Even if there were good roads and no obstacles, the journey along the coast is a long one and would require many days. But there are also rugged mountains to climb, wide marshes to cross, and dark forests to go through. There is hardly a footpath in all that wild region, nor any place to find rest or shelter. They say the woods are full of wild beasts, dreadful dragons lurk in the marshes, and many cruel robber giants dwell in the mountains."

"Well," said Theseus, "if there are more dangers by land than by sea, then I will go by land, and I go at once."

"But you will at least take fifty young men as companions with you?" asked his grandfather.

"No," said Theseus. "I go alone."

Then he kissed his mother and bade his grandfather good-bye, and left his home for the trackless coastland that lay to the west and north. With blessings and tears, his mother and grandfather followed him to the city gates, and watched him until his tall form was lost to sight among the trees that bordered the shore of the sea.

II. The Bed of Procrustes

With a brave heart, Theseus walked on, keeping the sea always upon his right. Soon he left behind the old city that was his home, and came to the great marshes, where the ground sank under him at every step, and green pools of stagnant water lay on both sides of the narrow path. No fiery

---

riddled: spread throughout
obstacles: challenges; things that get in the way
stagnant: stale; still; unmoving

dragon came out of the reeds to meet him, so he walked on and on until he came to the rugged mountain land.

For days he kept up a steady pace, till Athens was not more than twenty miles away. But now the road was only a narrow path winding among the rocks and up and down many a lonely wooded glen. Theseus had seen worse and more dangerous roads than this, and so he strode onward, happy in the thought that he was near the end of his long journey. But it was very slow traveling among the mountains, and he was not always sure that he was following the right path.

The sun was almost down when he came to a broad green valley where the trees had been cleared away. A little river flowed through the middle of this valley, and on either side were grassy meadows where cattle were grazing, and on a hillside close by, half hidden among the trees, there was a great stone house with vines running over its walls and roof.

While Theseus was wondering who it could be that lived in this pretty but lonely place, a man came out of the house and hurried down to the road to meet him. He was a well-dressed man, and his face was wreathed with smiles, and he bowed low to Theseus and invited him kindly to come up to the house and be his guest that night.

"This is a lonely place," he said, "and it is not often that travelers pass this way. But there is nothing that gives me so much joy as to find strangers and feast them at my table and hear them tell of the things they have seen and heard. Come, good sir, and sup with me, and lodge under my roof, and you shall sleep on a wonderful bed which I have—a bed that fits every guest and cures him of every ill."

---

glen: a small valley
wreathed: circled
sup: to eat supper; to dine

Theseus was pleased with the man's ways, and as he was both hungry and tired, he went up with him and sat down under the vines by the door. "Now," said the man, "I will go in and make the bed ready for you, and you can lie down upon it and rest. Later, when you feel refreshed, you shall sit at my table and sup with me, and I will listen to the pleasant tales I know you will tell."

When he had gone into the house, Theseus looked around him to see what sort of a place it was. He was filled with surprise at the richness of it—at the gold and silver and beautiful things with which every room seemed to be adorned—for it was indeed a place fit for a prince. While he was looking and wondering, the vines before him parted and the fair face of a young girl peeped out.

"Noble stranger," she whispered, "do not lie down on my master's bed, for those who do so never rise again. Fly down the glen and hide yourself in the deep woods before he returns, or else there will be no escape for you."

"Who is your master, fair maiden, that I should be afraid of him?" asked Theseus.

"Men call him Procrustes, or the Stretcher," said the girl, and she talked low and fast. "He is a robber. He brings hither all the strangers that he finds traveling through the mountains. He puts them on his iron bed, and robs them of all they have. No one who comes into his house ever goes out again."

"Why do they call him the Stretcher? And what is this iron bed of his?" asked Theseus.

"Did he not tell you that it fits all guests?" whispered the girl. "Most truly, it does fit them. For if a traveler is too long, Procrustes hews off his legs until he is the right length, but if

hither: here
hews: cuts

58

he is too short, as is the case with most guests, then the terrible bed stretches the poor traveler's limbs and body until he is long enough. That is why men call him the Stretcher. But hark! I hear him coming!" As the girl quickly withdrew, the vine leaves closed over her hiding-place.

The next moment, Procrustes stood in the door, bowing and smiling as though he had never done any harm to his fellow men. "My dear young friend," he said, "the bed is ready, and I will show you the way. After you have taken a pleasant little nap, we will sit down at table and you may tell me of the wonderful things you have seen in the course of your travels."

Theseus arose and followed his host, and when they had come into an inner chamber, there, surely enough, was the bed. The frame was made of iron, very curiously wrought, and upon it a soft mattress seemed to invite him to lie down and rest. But Theseus, peering about, saw the ax and the ropes with cunning pulleys lying hidden behind the curtains.

"Now, my dear young friend," said Procrustes, "I pray you lie down and take your ease, for I know that you have traveled far and are faint from want of rest. Lie down, and while sweet slumber overtakes you, I will take care that no disturbing noise, nor buzzing fly, nor vexing gnat disturbs your dreams."

"Is this your wonderful bed?" asked Theseus.

"It is," answered Procrustes, "and you need but to lie down upon it, and it will fit you perfectly."

"But you must lie upon it first," said Theseus, "and let me see how it will fit itself to your stature."

wrought: made
cunning: clever; crafty; tricky
vexing: annoying
stature: height

"Ah no," said Procrustes, "for then the spell would be broken," and as he spoke, his cheeks grew ashy pale.

"But I tell you, you must lie upon it," said Theseus, and he seized the man around the waist and threw him by force upon the bed. And no sooner was he prone upon the couch than curious iron arms reached out and clasped his body and held him so that he could not move hand or foot. The wretched man shrieked and cried for mercy, but Theseus stood over him and looked him straight in the eye.

"Is this the kind of hospitality you offer all your guests?" he asked.

Procrustes answered not a word. "Is it true," said Theseus, "that you have lured hundreds of travelers into your den only to rob them and make them fit your iron bed? Tell me, is this the awful truth?"

"It is true! It is true!" sobbed Procrustes, "and now kindly touch the spring above my head and let me go, and you shall have everything that I possess."

But Theseus turned away. "You are caught," he said, "in the trap you set for others and for me. Should there be mercy for the man who shows no mercy?" And Theseus went out of the room, and left Procrustes to the mercy of the terrible device.

Theseus looked through the house and found gold, silver, and many costly things that Procrustes had taken from the strangers who had fallen into his hands. He went into the dining hall, and there indeed was the table spread with a rich feast of meats and drinks and delicacies such as no king would scorn, but there was a seat and a plate for only the host, and none at all for guests.

---

delicacies: rare and delicious treats

Then the girl whose fair face Theseus had seen among the vines came running into the house. She seized the young hero's hands and thanked him warmly.

"Only a month ago," she cried, "my father, a rich merchant of Athens, was traveling, and I was with him, happy and carefree as any bird in the green woods. This robber lured us into his den, for we had much gold with us. My father, he stretched upon his iron bed, but me he made his slave."

Then Theseus called together all the people in the house, poor wretches whom Procrustes had forced to serve him, and he divided the robber's spoils among them and told them they were free to go wherever they wished.

In the morning, Theseus went on, through the narrow crooked ways among the mountains and hills. At last, he came to the plain of Athens, and gazed out over the noble city. And in its midst, he saw the white walls of the palace of the king.

III. HONOR AND HOME

As Theseus walked up the main street of the city, everyone wondered who the tall, fair youth could be. He continued straight to his father's palace.

"Where is the king?" he asked the guard.

"You cannot see the king," the guard answered, but, impressed by the noble bearing of the youth, he continued, "I will take you to his nephews."

The guard led the way into the feast hall, and there Theseus saw his fifty cousins sitting about the table, swilling

---

spoils: stolen items
swilling: drinking greedily

ale, arguing, and making great fools of themselves. As Theseus stood in the doorway, his teeth clenched in anger, one of the feasters saw him and cried out, "Well, tall stranger, what do you want here?"

Theseus only replied, "I am here to ask that hospitality which men should never refuse to give."

"Nor do we refuse," cried they. "Come in! Eat, drink, and be our guest."

"I will come in," said Theseus, "but I will be the guest of the king. Where is he?"

"Never mind the king," said one of the feasters. "Anyway, we hold the real power—if you want to get anything done here, you have to go through us."

Barely able to restrain his anger, Theseus strode boldly past the revelers and into the main halls of the palace, searching for the king. At last he found Aegeus, lonely and sad, sitting in an inner chamber. Theseus's heart broke to see the lines of care and worry upon the old man's face.

"Great king," he said gently, "I am a stranger in Athens and I have come to you to ask food and shelter and friendship such as I know you never deny."

"And who are you?" said the king.

"I am Theseus," answered the young man.

The king started and turned very pale—could this be the son whom he had so long hoped to see? His hands trembled as he felt his heart yearn strangely toward the young man. Then, checking himself, he said, "Yes! Yes! You are welcome, young hero, to such shelter and food and friendship as the King of Athens can give."

So, when the hour came, Theseus sat down to dine with the king, and while he ate he told of his deeds. He paused for

revelers: persons engaged in noisy partying

a moment in his talk to help himself to a piece of the roasted meat, and as was the custom of the time, drew his sword to carve it. As the sword flashed from its scabbard, Aegeus saw the letters engraved upon it—the initials of his name. And he knew at once that it was the sword he had hidden so many years before under the stone on the mountainside by the city beyond the sea.

"My son! My son!" he cried, and he sprang up and flung his arms around Theseus. It was indeed a glad meeting for both father and son, and they had many things to ask and to tell.

The very next morning, Aegeus sent out his heralds to make it known all through the city that his son Theseus had arrived, and that he would in time be king in his stead. When the fifty nephews heard this, they were angry and alarmed.

"Shall this upstart cheat us out of our heritage?" they cried, and they made a plot to ambush Theseus in a grove close by the city gate.

Very cunningly did the wicked fellows lay their trap to catch the young hero. One morning, as he was passing that way alone, several of them fell suddenly upon him with swords and lances, and tried to slay him outright. They were thirty to one, but he faced them boldly and held them at bay, while he shouted for help. The men of Athens, who had borne so many wrongs at the hands of the greedy nephews, came running out from the streets. In the fight that followed, every one of the plotters was slain, and the other nephews, when they heard about it, fled from the city and never returned.

---

in his stead: in his place
upstart: a person who acts more important than he or she really is
heritage: something that one inherits

IV. The Black-Sailed Ship

For months, all the people of Athens were glad, for brave Theseus had come to live among them, and they felt confident that when his time came to rule, he would rule them well. But when the springtime came again, the doors of all the houses were shut and no man went in or out, but all sat silent with pale cheeks. A black-sailed ship stood ominously in the harbor, and a host of rude soldiers from Crete appeared, parading in the streets, shouting, "Hear us, all Athenians! In three days, your tribute will be due and must be paid!"

"What is the meaning of all this?" cried Theseus to the king. "Why do all look so fearfully at the black-sailed ship in the harbor? And what right does a Cretan have to demand tribute in Athens?"

With tears in his eyes, King Aegeus took the young prince aside and said, "Shortly after you were born, King Minos of Crete made war on Athens. When I heard the news, I hid the sword and sandals underneath the great stone, and then returned here at once. It was then I learned that some of your nephews had killed King Minos's only son and then spread the story that I had done it. They hoped that Minos would kill me so that one of them might become king."

"A foul and wicked deed!" cried Theseus.

"Minos came with all his army to avenge the death of his son," Aegeus continued. "He laid waste to the land, set fire to our ships, and surrounded the city. We asked for peace. He agreed, but in return for not destroying our city, he demanded a terrible tribute. Each year, seven youths and

---

host: a great many
tribute: in this usage, payment from one nation to another
avenge: to get revenge for; to get even for

seven maidens must board the black-sailed ship and journey from Athens to Crete. There they are given to the Minotaur, a monster half-man and half-bull, that roams in the Labyrinth, a maze of rooms and corridors beneath the city.

"It is better," Aegeus sobbed, "that a few should die, even in so terrible a way, than all should be destroyed. I can say no more."

"But I will say more!" cried Theseus. "Athens shall not pay tribute to Crete. I myself will go with these youths and maidens, and I will slay the Minotaur and defy King Minos himself upon his throne."

"Oh, do not be so rash!" said the king, "for no one who is thrust into the Labyrinth ever comes out again. Remember that you are the hope of Athens. Do not take this great risk upon yourself."

"You say that I am the hope of Athens," said Theseus. "How then can I do anything but go?" And he began at once to make himself ready.

Three days later, all the youths and maidens of the city were brought together in the marketplace, so that lots might be cast for those who were to be taken. Two vessels of brass were brought and set before King Aegeus and the herald who had come from Crete. Into one vessel they placed as many glass beads as there were noble young men in the city, and into the other as many as there were maidens. All the beads were white except seven in each vessel, and those were as black as ebony.

Then every maiden, without looking, reached her hand into one of the vessels and drew forth a bead, and those who drew the black beads were taken away to the black-sailed ship. The young men drew lots in the same way, but when

defy: to challenge or confront

six black beads had been drawn, Theseus came forward and said, "Hold! Let no more beads be drawn. I will be the seventh youth to pay this tribute. Now let us go aboard the black-sailed ship and be off."

Then the people and King Aegeus went down to the shore to take leave of the young men and maidens, whom they had no hope of seeing again. And all but Theseus wept and were brokenhearted.

"Father," said Theseus to the king, "do not weep. I will return."

"I hope that you may," said the old king. "And if when this ship returns, I see a white sail spread above the black one, then I shall know that you are alive and well, but if I see only the black one, it will tell me that you have perished."

And now the vessel was loosed from its mooring, the north wind filled the sail, and the seven youths and seven maidens were borne away over the sea, toward the dreadful fate that awaited them on the isle of Crete.

V. THE PRINCESS AND THE LABYRINTH

When the ship reached Crete, the young people were set ashore. A party of soldiers led them through the streets toward the prison where they were to stay until morning. They did not weep, but with pale faces and firm-set lips they walked between the rows of houses, and looked neither to the right nor to the left. The windows and doors were full of people who were eager to see them.

"What a pity that such brave young men should be food for the Minotaur," muttered some.

"Ah, how awful that maidens so fair should meet a fate so sad!" sighed others.

Then they passed by the palace gate, where stood King Minos and his daughter, Ariadne.

"Indeed, those are noble young fellows," said the king.

"Yes, too noble to feed to the vile Minotaur," said Ariadne.

"The nobler, the better," said the king grimly. "For not one of them can compare with your lost brother."

Ariadne said no more, but she thought that she had never seen anyone who looked so much like a hero as young Theseus. How brave he was, how proud his eye, how firm his step!

That night, Ariadne made a plan to set Theseus and his companions free. At the earliest peep of day she arose, while everyone else was asleep. She ran out of the palace and hurried to the prison. Since she was the king's daughter, the jailer opened the door at her bidding and allowed her to go in.

There sat the seven youths and the seven maidens on the ground, but they had not lost hope. She took Theseus aside and thrust a sword into his hand.

"Take this sword," she whispered, "for only with it can you hope to slay the Minotaur. And here is a ball of silken thread. As soon as you go into the Labyrinth, fasten one end of the thread to the stone doorpost, and unwind it as you go along. When you have slain the Minotaur, follow the thread and it will lead you back to the door. In the meantime, I will make sure that your ship is ready to sail. Then I will wait for you at the door of the Labyrinth."

"Thank you, princess," said Theseus. "If I live to return to Athens, then it is my wish that you will return with me and be my bride."

Ariadne clasped his hands and smiled, and then she hastened away.

---

vile: foul; repulsive; horrible

As soon as the sun was up, the guards came to lead the young prisoners to the Labyrinth. They did not see the sword Theseus hid behind him, nor the ball of silk that he held in his closed hand and tied swiftly to the doorpost as they entered.

The guards led the youths and maidens a long way into the Labyrinth, turning here and there, back and forth, a thousand different times, until it seemed certain that they could never find their way out again. Then, by a secret passage that they alone knew, the guards went out and left them, as they had left many others before, to wander about until the Minotaur found them.

"Do not fear," said Theseus to his companions. "Stay close to me, and I will protect you." And under his breath he whispered, "Athena, help and guard me!"

Then he drew his sword and stood in the narrow hall before them. For hours they waited, hearing no sound, seeing no shadow. At last, late in the day, they heard a bellowing, low and faint and far away. They listened and soon heard it again, a little louder, and very fierce and dreadful.

"The monster approaches!" cried Theseus. "Now for the fight!"

Then he shouted so loudly that the walls of the Labyrinth answered back, and the sound was carried upward to the sky and outward to the rocks and cliffs of the mountains. The Minotaur heard him, and his bellowing grew louder and fiercer every moment.

Theseus ran forward to meet the beast. The Minotaur came into view, rushing down the passage. He was twice as tall as a man, and his head was like a bull's with huge horns, fiery eyes, and a mouth as large and sharp as a lion's. When he saw Theseus with the sword in his hand coming to meet him, he paused, for no one had ever faced him in that way before. Then he put his head down and rushed forward, roaring furiously. At the last second, Theseus leaped aside and made a sharp thrust with his sword into the monster's leg as he passed.

The Minotaur fell upon the ground, groaning and beating wildly about with his horned head and his hoof-like fists. Theseus ran up and thrust the sword into the creature's heart. He was away again before the beast could harm him, and soon the Minotaur turned his face to the sky and lay dead.

The youths and maidens ran to Theseus, weeping and thanking him, but Theseus only said, "Come, let us hurry.

Follow me as I wind up the silken thread, and we will find our way out of this gruesome Labyrinth."

Through a thousand rooms and courts and winding ways they went. At midnight, they came at last to the outer door and saw the city lying in the moonlight before them. Only a little way off was the seashore where the black-sailed ship that had brought them to Crete was moored. There stood Ariadne, waiting for them.

"The wind is fair, and the sea is smooth," she whispered to Theseus as she took his arm.

---

gruesome: horrible, usually as the result of some terrible violence

When the morning dawned they were far out to sea, and looking back from the deck of the little vessel, only the white tops of the Cretan mountains were in sight. And when King Minos arose and found his daughter gone, he tore his hair and cried, "Now indeed, I am bereft of all my treasures."

In the meantime, King Aegeus of Athens stayed day after day on a high tower by the shore, hoping to see a ship coming from the south. At last, the vessel with Theseus and his companions came in sight. But it still carried only the black sail, for in their haste and joy, the young men had forgotten to raise the white one.

"Alas! Alas! My son has perished!" moaned Aegeus, and he fainted and fell forward into the sea and was drowned. Thus did sadness cast a shadow on the joy of the homecoming of Theseus and the Athenian youths and maidens.

Theseus became king of Athens. He ruled the city wisely and well. One of his first commands was to order that in the harbor a monument be built to the memory of his father. And that sea, even to this day, has been called by the name of the good old king, the Aegean Sea.

---

bereft: deprived or robbed

JASON AND THE GOLDEN FLEECE

I. CHIRON

Long ago, the sun rose over the kingdom of Iolcos and shone upon an old man leading his little son by the hand into the misty mountains. Farther and farther they walked, over marsh and crag, and across rushing rivers, until the boy could walk no more and the old man had to carry him.

At last, near the top of the oldest mountain of them all, they stopped at the mouth of a lonely cave. The old man put the boy down and whispered, "Do not fear, but go inside, and whomever you find, lay your hands on his knees and say, 'Please take me as your guest and student from this day forth.'"

The boy went inside without trembling. And there was Chiron, the ancient centaur, wisest of all creatures beneath the sky. From head to waist he was a man, but below he had the legs and body of a horse. His hair rolled down over his broad shoulders, his beard curled over his brown chest, and

---

crag: a rugged cliff

his dark, mild eyes seemed to glow with a soft light. He held a golden lyre, and when the boy entered, he struck it and began to sing:

> *The mountain is high,*
> *The sea is deep,*
> *The strife of kings*
> *Makes all men weep.*
> *Go, hero bold,*
> *Into the world*
> *And bring ye back*
> *The prize of peace.*

The boy listened in wonder. When the song ended, he ran to the centaur and would have laid his hands upon his knees, but Chiron said, "Call your father inside, Jason, for I know he is here, too."

When the old man had come inside the cave, Chiron said, "Welcome, O king. But, tell me, why did you not come in yourself?"

The king replied, "I thought you would pity Jason if he came alone. And I wanted to know if he would act like a king's son and show no fear."

Then he bowed his head and said, "Pelias the terrible has stolen my throne. Now he rules as king of Iolcos. I beg you, Chiron, keep Jason here with you so that Pelias cannot hurt him, and train him to be a great man so that he can one day win back our throne and become king."

---

lyre: a musical instrument like a small harp
strife: conflict; struggle

Chiron nodded. Then turning to Jason, he said, "Are you afraid of my horse's hooves, or will you be my student from this day forth?"

"I would gladly have horse's hooves, too," replied the boy, "if I could sing a song like yours."

Chiron laughed. "Sit here by me until sundown," he said. "Then your playfellows will come home, and like them you shall learn to be a king, worthy to rule over gallant men."

To the king, he said, "Go home in peace, and bend before the storm like a prudent man. Jason shall not cross the river again until he has become a glory to you and your house."

The king went sadly home, but Jason was too excited to weep, for Chiron put the golden lyre into his hands and began to teach him how to play. And when the sun sank low behind the mountain, the rocks rang with the shouts of boys returning from the day's hunt, and Chiron and Jason leapt up and hurried outside to greet them.

There waited the young heroes: Aeneas, Hercules, Peleus, and many others with great names. Each showed the prize he had taken that day—a deer or a bear or a mountain lion—all but one, who stood a little way off from the others with his arms full of herbs and flowers, and a spotted snake curled around his wrist. His name was Asclepius, and of him Chiron said, "Each person is given some gift, and each gift is worthy in its place. But while others have been given the skill to kill in the hunt, Asclepius has been given an honor beyond all honors: the power to cure."

Then the lads brought in wood and split it and lit a blazing fire. While their supper cooked, they washed in a

gallant: spirited; brave
prudent: exercising good judgment and caution

stream that ran beside the cave. Then they ate until they could eat no more, drank the clear spring water, and took turns singing and playing Chiron's golden lyre. After a while, they went out to a plot of grass at the cave's mouth, where they ran and wrestled and laughed until the stones fell from the cliffs. That night, Jason went eagerly to bed, waiting for the morrow when he would join his fellows in learning to be a king.

II. The River and the Kingdom

For ten years, Jason studied with Chiron. He grew up strong and brave and wise. At last, one day he stood alone with the centaur on the mountaintop. As he looked out over the mountains and the towns and the sea and the plains, he wondered what place he would take in the world of men.

"Is it true what the heroes tell me, that I am heir of the kingdom of Iolcos?" he asked.

"And what good would it be to you if you were?" answered the centaur.

"I would take my kingdom back and keep it, and bring honor to my name."

"A strong man has taken it and kept it long. Are you stronger than Pelias the terrible?"

"I am," said Jason. "But there is no glory in that until all the world knows it."

Chiron sighed. "You will face many dangers before you rule in Iolcos," he said, "such as no man has ever seen before."

"Then I will be happy," replied Jason. "For what is better than to see what no man has ever seen before?"

Chiron nodded. "The eaglet must leave the nest when it is fledged," he said. "But promise me two things: speak harshly to no one, and always keep your word."

Jason promised, and then, with a joyful yell, he ran down the mountainside.

Down he went through the thickets and forests until he came to the raging river Anauros. But so great had been the summer flood that the boulders shuddered like galloping horses. They shook the rocks on which Jason stood and tossed the swirling waters into mountains of white foam.

On the riverbank stood a wrinkled old woman. When she saw Jason, she whined, "Will you carry me across the river? You are young and strong, and I am old and weak. For Hera's sake, carry me over the torrent."

Jason was going to answer scornfully, but then he remembered Chiron's words and said, "For Hera's sake, I will carry you across the torrent, unless we are both drowned along the way."

Then the old woman leapt upon his back, and Jason staggered into the river. The first step was up to his knees. The second step was up to his waist. And as his feet slipped on the stones, the old woman cried, "Boy, you have gotten my mantle wet! Shame on you for playing such a game with an old woman like me."

Jason had half a mind to drop her, and let her get through the torrent by herself. But he remembered Chiron's words and said only, "Patience, my lady. Even the best horse may stumble some day."

---

fledged: grown to the point of independence
torrent: swiftly flowing water
mantle: a cloak

Jason struggled bravely through the wild waters, and at last stepped onto the shore. As he set the old woman down, he noticed he had lost one of his sandals. He gazed out over the surface of the roiling river and searched along the shore, but it was nowhere to be seen.

Then he turned to speak to the old woman. But as he looked at her, she grew fairer than all women, and taller than all men on earth. Her garments shone like the summer sea, and her jewels sparkled like stars. Over her forehead was a veil woven of the golden clouds of sunset, and through the veil she looked down on him with great soft eyes.

She said, "I am Hera, Queen of Mount Olympus. As you have done to me, so will I do to you. Call on me in your hour of need, and I will not forget you."

Then she disappeared, and, with new courage, Jason continued on his journey.

When Jason reached Iolcos, all the people came out to look at him. Some of the elders whispered together, and finally one of them stopped him and said, "Fair lad, who are you, where do you come from, and why have you come to Iolcos?"

"My name is Jason," he replied. "I come from Chiron's cave in the mountains, and I am here to see Pelias the terrible."

The elder started and shook his head. "Do you dare to go so boldly through town with only one sandal? Do you not know the word of the oracle?"

"I am a stranger here, and know of no oracle," Jason replied. "But what of my sandal? I lost it as I crossed the river Anauros."

---

roiling: stirred up; churning

oracle: in mythology, a being who was believed to have knowledge from the gods

The old man sighed and said, "I will tell you, for it could mean your death if I do not. Beware how you speak at Pelias's palace, for he is the cruelest and most cunning of kings, and the oracle at Delphi has said that a man wearing one sandal will take the kingdom from Pelias and keep it for himself."

Then Jason laughed a great laugh. "Good news," he said, "for both you and me. That is exactly why I have come."

And he strode on toward the palace, while all the people wondered at his noble bearing.

III. The Quest for the Golden Fleece

When Jason arrived at the palace, he stood in the doorway and cried, "Come out, Pelias. Come and fight me for your kingdom."

Pelias came to the door in a rage. But when he saw that Jason wore only one sandal, his face turned from red to white, and he said only, "Who are you, brazen youth?"

"I am Jason, son of the true king, and the heir of all this land."

Pelias was not brave, but he was very clever. He lifted up his hands and eyes and wept, or seemed to weep. "What joy!" he cried. "I have three daughters, but no son to be my heir. You shall be my heir, and rule the kingdom after me, and marry whichever of my daughters you choose. Now come in, come in, and feast with me," and he led Jason inside.

While they feasted, Jason said to Pelias, "I find you kind and hospitable, and as you are to me, so I will be to you. But

---

bearing: manner; the way one carries oneself
brazen: bold and daring
hospitable: generous with guests

men say that you are terrible and cruel, and drove my father out of Iolcos."

"Lies, all lies," sighed Pelias. "Your father was growing old and weary. He gave me the kingdom himself. You shall see him tomorrow, and ask him. He will tell you the same thing."

Jason's heart leapt. "My father?" he cried. "Ah, you must be true-hearted indeed to keep such a great man beside you."

Pelias flinched. "How could I do otherwise?" he said lightly. Then he cocked his head and said, "And I can see that you will be an even greater king than your father."

"I would do anything for the glory of the kingdom and my father's house," said Jason.

"Anything?" asked Pelias casually.

"Anything!" Jason affirmed eagerly.

"Would you, indeed?" said Pelias. His eyes narrowed. "In the kingdom of Colchis, there is a golden ram's fleece that rightfully belongs to us. Go and fetch it. It should not be too great a task for a bold young hero like you. And when you return, you shall marry one of my daughters, and I will make you king of Iolcos."

All the court gasped. For they understood, as did Jason, that to go on such a quest meant almost certain doom, as the Golden Fleece, which lay far beyond the uncharted seas, was guarded by terrible monsters and kept by a powerful king.

Jason clenched his teeth and thought, "If I do not go, I will be dishonored. But if I do go, I may never return." Then he sprang to his feet, furious that he had allowed himself to be trapped by the smooth words of Pelias. But, remembering his promise to Chiron, he replied, "You have spoken well,

flinched: drew back quickly in fear, pain, or surprise
affirmed: agreed

cunning king! I
love glory, and I
dare keep my
word. I will go and
fetch the Golden
Fleece. Only
promise me this in
return: treat my
father well while I
am gone, and give
me the kingdom
for my own on the
day that I bring
back the Golden
Fleece."

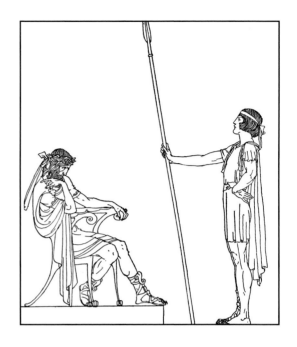

Pelias was silent for a moment. "I promise," he said
quietly, "for it will be no shame to give up my kingdom to
the man who wins that fleece."

That night, Jason could not sleep. "How will I fulfill my
promise?" he wondered. "I have no wealth and no friends
in Iolcos."

Then he seemed to see Hera's soft eyes, and at once, he
had an idea.

The next morning, he went before Pelias and said, "If you
truly want me to win the Golden Fleece, send two heralds
out to call the princes who were students of Chiron with me,
and we will go together upon the quest."

And Pelias sent the heralds at once, for he said to himself,
"Let all the princes go with him, and, like him, never return.
Then I will make myself king of all Greece."

So that day and many of the next, from the mountains to the sea, the land rang with the heralds' cry, "Who dares come on the Adventure of the Golden Fleece?"

All the heroes' hearts were stirred, and they came from their homes and palaces to Iolcos. First came Hercules the mighty, with his lion's skin and club, and behind him Hylas his young squire, who bore his arrows and his bow. Then Peleus came, and the healer, Asclepius, and Argus, the famed shipbuilder. Fifty heroes came in all, wearing helmets of brass and gold with tall dyed horsehair crests, embroidered shirts of linen beneath their coats of mail, and greaves of polished tin to guard their legs in battle. Each carried a shield upon his shoulder, a sword of tempered bronze in his silver-studded belt, and in his right hand a pair of lances made of heavy white ash.

All the city came out to meet the heroes. Never before had there been such a gathering, and all the people wondered if there ever would be again, or if the heroes would be lost on this terrible quest.

IV. Orpheus and the *Argo*

To reach Colchis, where the Golden Fleece was kept, the heroes needed a mighty ship. So together they felled the pines around Iolcos, and the wise shipwright Argus taught them to build a galley, the first long ship that ever sailed the seas. He showed them how to bore holes for fifty oars, one for each hero of the crew. He helped them fill the cracks with pitch and paint the bow all in scarlet, and for that, they named the ship *Argo* after him.

mail: armor made of metal plates or rings
greaves: protective armor for the shins
tempered: hardened

While they built, Jason journeyed through the north until he found Orpheus, prince of minstrels. "Old friend," said Jason, "will you sail with me to Colchis to win the Golden Fleece, and charm all the men and monsters we meet with your lyre and song?"

"I have wandered far and wide since I lived in Chiron's cave," replied Orpheus, "and I am weary of travel. But I will go with you for friendship's sake, and help you win back your kingdom."

Jason and Orpheus returned to Iolcos, where the heroes had just finished building the ship. Together, they tried to launch it into the sea, but the boat was too heavy for them to move, and the keel sank deep into the sand. But Jason said, "Let Orpheus play upon his lyre. Perhaps his song can succeed where our strength cannot."

Then Orpheus picked up his harp and sang:

> *How sweet it is to ride upon the surges,*
> *To leap from wave to wave,*
> *While the wind sings cheerful in the cordage.*
> *How sweet it is to roam across the ocean,*
> *And see new towns and wondrous lands,*
> *To come home laden with treasure,*
> *And win undying fame!*

And the *Argo* heard him, and longed to be away and out at sea. Every plank stirred and the ship heaved from stem to

---

minstrels: in ancient times, singers of verses, often about heroes and their deeds
keel: the part of the boat that juts out from the bottom
surges: large waves
cordage: the ropes of a ship's rigging

stern. The heroes quickly laid out a path of pine trunks before it, and the ship rolled over them into the waiting sea.

They stored the ship well with food and water, then pulled the ladder up on board. Each man took his oar, and rowed in time with Orpheus's song. The people lined the cliffs, and the women waved and the men shouted at the starting of the gallant crew.

V. The Secret

After much sailing, the heroes brought the *Argo* to rest on a cold and windswept beach. They walked through a forest of storm-whipped trees to the silent, empty city beyond. "What happened here?" they muttered to each other.

A sad-faced man met them at the palace doors and said, "Welcome, heroes; I am King Phineus. This was once a golden land, glowing with grain and riches. Now it is a land of bitterness and misery, bare as the rocks that line the beach. Yet come in, and I will show you what hospitality I can."

He led them into the palace, and set meat and drink before them. But before they could even taste the food, two monsters flew in through the window. They had the faces and hair of fair maidens, but the wings and claws of hawks. They snatched the food off of the table, and flew shrieking around the room, sending off icy whirlwinds with each beat of their enormous wings.

"What are those beasts?" cried Jason. "What do they want?"

"They are Harpies," replied King Phineus. "They sweep the food off of our tables and ravage our beaches with storms so that we starve in spite of all our wealth."

Furious, two of the heroes sprang up and chased the Harpies out of the room, through the city and along the beach. So fierce was their battle that every building, from the meanest hut to the palace itself, swayed on its foundations. Great stones were torn from the crags, and the forest pines were hurled earthward. The sea boiled white with foam, and the clouds were dashed against the cliffs. But at last the Harpies fled screaming toward the south.

"How can I thank you?" cried the king. "My treasures are gone and my kingdom is worthless. But I do have one thing that you might find valuable: a secret. If you are truly sailing to Colchis, you must beware the Clashing Rocks. Every ship that tries to sail through is smashed between them. But I know the secret for passing through safely, and I will tell it to you."

---

ravage: to destroy; to bring to ruin
meanest: poorest

Phineus explained the secret, and then the heroes hurried to their ship and set sail. Soon they saw the Clashing Rocks shining like spires of gray glass. As they neared, they could see them heaving and rolling upon the long sea-waves, crashing and grinding together.

Then Jason took out a dove that Phineus had given him. "Fear not," he said, as he released it into the air, "this bird will be our pilot."

The dove rushed through the rocks like an arrow, and the rocks clashed together around it. But the bird was so swift that the rocks only struck one feather from its tail, and then sprang apart in shock.

The heroes cheered and paddled madly to rush through the toppling ice-crags. But the Clashing Rocks were stuck apart, and clashed neither around them nor any ship since to this day.

VI. The Kingdom of Colchis

The heroes sailed south until at last they arrived at the burning beach of Colchis. They strode from the beach into the city, and the king rode out in his chariot to meet them. His robes were made of heavy gold cloth, and his diadem flashed like lightning. In his hand, he held a jeweled scepter, which glittered like the stars. He looked at them sternly and said, "Who are you, and what business have you here? I warn you, my people have never yet tired in battle, and we know well how to rid ourselves of an army as small as yours."

Jason answered, "We are not pirates or lawless men. We come only to bring home our Golden Fleece. And these, my

spires: tall, narrow towers
diadem: a crown, like a headband

bold comrades, are no nameless men. They are heroes, who also never tire in battle, and know well how to give blows and to take. Yet we wish to be guests at your table, for it will be better that way for us both."

The king's eyes flashed fire, but he said, "You wish to take away the Golden Fleece without a fight? Very well. Choose the best man among you, and let him fulfill the labors I demand. If he succeeds, I will give him the Golden Fleece for a prize."

That evening, as Jason sat by the sea, planning how he might fulfill the labors and win the Golden Fleece, the king's daughter, Medea, crept out from the reeds and stood beside him.

"Go home," she said to Jason. "You do not know what the man who wishes to win the fleece must do. He must tame two bronze-footed bulls that breathe fire, and make them plow four acres. Then he must sow the furrows with serpents' teeth. But from each tooth will spring an armed warrior, and he must fight and conquer them all. If he is successful even in that, the fleece is guarded by a dragon as big as your ship, and he must step over its body to reach it."

Jason laughed bitterly. "Unjustly is that fleece kept here, and by an unjust and lawless king. So unjustly will I die, for I will attempt it before another sun sets."

"If you fear nothing, why should you die?" said Medea, trembling. "I can help you win the Golden Fleece." Jason's eyes glittered as she continued, "I have an ointment here. If you anoint yourself with it, you will have the strength of seven men, and if you anoint your shield with it, neither fire

comrades: friends
furrows: the trenches left in a field after plowing
anoint: to rub with oil or ointment

nor sword can harm you. Anoint your helmet with it before you sow the serpents' teeth, and when the warriors spring up out of the ground, cast your helmet in among them, and the field will mow itself and perish."

Then Jason fell on his knees before her, and thanked her and kissed her hands, and she gave him the vase of ointment, and fled into the reeds. At sunrise Jason bathed, and anointed himself from head to foot, and anointed his shield, his helmet, and his weapons.

Then the heroes went to the king of Colchis and said, "Fulfill your promise to us. Give us the serpents' teeth, and let loose the fiery bulls; for we have found a champion among us who can win the Golden Fleece."

The king glared at them, but he could not go back on his promise. So he gave them the serpents' teeth. Then he called for his chariot and horses, and sent heralds through the town, and all the people went with him to the dreadful field.

Then Jason cried, "Let the fiery bulls come forth."

The king ordered the gates opened, and the bulls leapt out. Their bronze hoofs rang upon the ground, and their nostrils sent out sheets of flame as they rushed with lowered heads upon Jason. But Jason did not move an inch. The flame of their breath swept round him, but the ointment prevented it from burning even a single hair on his head.

He sprang upon the nearest, and seized him by the horns. Up and down they wrestled, until the bull fell to his knees. In a moment, he had tamed the second and yoked them both to the plow, and goaded them on with his lance until they had plowed the entire field.

---

goaded: urged to action; prodded

Then he sowed the serpents' teeth in the furrows and waited. And Medea looked at him and at his helmet, so that he would not forget the instructions she had given him.

Soon, smoke began to rise from the field. Every furrow began to heave and bubble. Then, out of every clod of dirt rose a warrior clad from head to foot in armor. As one, they drew their swords and rushed on Jason, where he stood in the midst of them, alone.

The heroes were wide-eyed with fear, and the king laughed and said, "See! If I had not warriors enough already round me, I could even call them out of the earth."

But Jason snatched off his helmet, and hurled it into the thickest of the throng. And one cried to his fellow, "You struck me. You must die!" To which the other replied, "Nay, you must die!" Then, as fury seized the earth-born phantoms, each turned his hand against the rest, and they fought until they all lay still upon the ground. Then the magic furrows opened, and the kind earth took them home, and the grass grew green again above them, and Jason's work was done.

VII. THE ESCAPE

The heroes cheered, and Jason cried, "Lead me to the fleece this moment, before the sun goes down."

But the king thought, "He has conquered the bulls, and sown and reaped the deadly crop. He very well may kill the dragon. But how could he know our secrets?"

Then he turned to Medea. "This is your doing, isn't it, my daughter? False maid, you have helped these yellow-haired strangers and brought shame upon us!"

Medea shrank back, and she could not meet the king's eyes. The king knew that she was guilty and hissed, "If they win the fleece, you will die."

To the heroes, he said, "We will decide in the morning, when you shall face the dragon that guards the Golden Fleece."

But as the heroes marched back to the *Argo*, they growled like lions cheated out of their prey. One of them said, "This king will never let us face the dragon and try to win the Golden Fleece. So let us go to the grove together tonight and take the fleece by force."

Said another, "Yes, we can draw lots for who shall go in first. While the dragon is devouring one, the rest can slay him and carry off the fleece." But Jason held them back, for he hoped for Medea's help.

When darkness fell, Medea slipped out from the shadows and cried, "My father has found out that I have helped you. Go home, go home, for my end is near."

"You need not die," said Jason. "Flee with us across the sea. Show us how to win the fleece, and come with us. You shall be my queen, and rule with me in Iolcos by the sea."

But Medea wept. "Must I leave my home and my people, to wander with strangers across the sea?" she said between sobs. "Ah, I cast my lot, and I must endure it. I will show you how to win the Golden Fleece. Bring up your ship by the woods, and moor her there against the bank. Come up at midnight, and Orpheus with you, for I hear that he is the king of all minstrels, and can charm all things on earth."

And Orpheus laughed for joy, and clapped his hands, because the choice had fallen on him. For in those days poets and singers were as bold warriors as the best.

cast my lot: an expression meaning "made my choice"

So at midnight they went up the bank, and Medea led them through the wood to where the Golden Fleece hung upon a tree. Jason would have sprung to seize it, but Medea held him back, and pointed where the dragon lay. His body was like a mountain-pine. His coils stretched many fathoms, and were spangled with bronze and gold.

When he saw them coming, he lifted up his head, and watched them with his small bright eyes. He flashed his forked tongue and roared until the forest swayed and

---

fathoms: units of six feet, usually used to measure the depth of water

groaned. But Medea called gently to him, and he stretched out his long spotted neck, and licked her hand, and looked up in her face, as if asking for food. Then she made a sign to Orpheus, and he began his song.

As he sang, the forest grew calm again, and the leaves on every tree hung still. The serpent's head sank down, his brazen coils grew limp, and his glittering eyes closed lazily, until he breathed as gently as a child.

Then Jason crept forward and stepped over the sleeping dragon. He tore the fleece from off the tree-trunk, and rushed with Orpheus and Medea back through the woods, to the safety of the *Argo*'s deck.

Jason lifted the Golden Fleece, and all the heroes gazed at it silently as it glowed in the light of the moon. Then he cried, "Go now, good *Argo*, swift and steady, if ever you want to see Iolcos again."

And she went, as the heroes drove her, grim and silent, with muffled oars, till the pinewood bent like willow in their hands. The stout *Argo* groaned beneath their strokes.

The homeward journey of the heroes took them to unknown seas and new dangers—and alas, from these perils, some of the heroes did not return. When at long last the *Argo* came to the shores of Iolcos, the exhausted heroes crawled onto the beach, and some sat down and wept as they thought of the gallant comrades they had lost.

Then Jason went up to the palace. There he found Pelias, sitting by the hearth, crippled and blind with age, while opposite him sat Jason's father, also crippled and blind.

And Jason fell down at his father's knees, and wept, and called him by his name. And the old man stretched out his hands, and felt him, and said, "Do not mock me, young hero. My son Jason is dead long ago at sea."

"I am your own son, Jason, whom you trusted to Chiron in the mountains. I have brought home the Golden Fleece. I have fulfilled my promise, and have come at last to reclaim our kingdom."

Then his father clung to him like a child, and wept, and would not let him go, as he cried, "Now I shall not go down lonely to my grave. Promise never to leave me till I die."

And so, in joy mixed with grief, ended the quest of Jason and the Argonauts for the Golden Fleece.

---

mock: to ridicule; to make fun of meanly

TALES OF LOVE AND FRIENDSHIP

BAUCIS AND PHILEMON

On a certain hill in a far-distant country there are two beautiful trees, a linden and an oak. At the foot of the hill there is an ugly marsh, and a little farther away there is a lake. A wonderful story is told about the trees and the lake.

One evening old Philemon and his old wife, Baucis, sat at their cottage door, enjoying the beautiful sunset. They had just eaten their frugal supper and intended now to spend a quiet hour or two before bedtime. So they talked together about their garden, and their cow, and their grapevine on the cottage wall. But the rude shouts of children and the sharp barking of dogs in the village nearby grew louder and louder. At last it became hard for Baucis and Philemon to hear each other speak.

"Ah, wife," cried Philemon, "I fear some poor traveler is seeking shelter among our neighbors in the village. Instead of giving him food and lodging, they have set the dogs after him."

"I do wish," answered old Baucis, "that our neighbors were a little more kindly. Think of bringing up children in this wicked way—they even pat them on the head when they fling stones at strangers!"

"I never heard the dogs bark so loudly before," said the good old man.

"Nor the children shout such rude things," answered his good old wife.

---

frugal: having or using only just enough; simple, without luxury

"Those children will come to no good," said Philemon, shaking his white head. "To tell you the truth, wife, I would not be surprised if some terrible thing were to happen to all the people in the village, unless they mend their ways. But as for you and me, as long as we have a crust of bread, let us be ready to give half to any poor stranger that may come along and need it."

"Yes, dear husband, so we will," said Baucis.

They sat shaking their heads, while the noise grew nearer and nearer. Soon, at the foot of the little hill on which their cottage stood, they saw two travelers approaching. Close behind them came the fierce dogs snarling at their heels. A little way off ran a crowd of children who sent up shrill cries and flung stones at the strangers with all their might. Once or twice the younger of the two men turned and drove back the dogs with a staff he carried in his hand. His companion, who was a very tall person, walked calmly along.

Both of the travelers were humbly clad. They looked as if they had not money enough in their pockets to pay for a night's lodging.

"Come, wife," said Philemon to Baucis, "let us go and meet these poor people."

"You go and meet them," answered Baucis, "while I make haste within to get them something for supper."

So she hurried into the cottage, while Philemon went forward and extended his hand, saying, "Welcome! Come in and rest yourselves. Come in, and my wife, Baucis, will give you some food, for I know that you are tired and hungry."

The strangers followed the old man into the hut. Philemon gave them seats just inside the door, as Baucis hurried to prepare some food for them. The good woman had raked out

humbly clad: dressed simply and plainly

the coals that lay among the ashes on the hearth and laid some dry sticks upon them, so there was a blazing fire. From the garden she had gathered some fresh vegetables. She cut a slice of meat from the side of bacon that hung in the chimney corner, and filled the great dinner pot that swung above the flames.

While the food was cooking she drew out a little table and covered it with a snow-white cloth. On the bench where her guests were to sit she placed a cushion filled with soft and fragrant seaweed. Then she placed on the table sweet-smelling herbs, radishes, cheese, and eggs cooked in the ashes.

When all was ready, the stew, smoking hot, was dipped from the kettle and served in coarse earthen dishes. Some milk was served from a yellow pitcher, and apples and wild honey were added for dessert. But better than all these were the kind faces of Baucis and Philemon—their looks of welcome, their attention to every need of their unknown visitors. The guests sat down at the table and the good old people stood behind them, ready to serve them and satisfy their wants.

"Kind Mother Baucis," said the younger of the travelers, "a little more milk, if you please. This day has been hot, and I am very thirsty."

"Oh dear!" cried Baucis. "I am sorry and ashamed, but the truth is, there is not a drop left in the pitcher. Oh, had I known you were coming, we would have gone without milk at our supper!"

"It appears to me," said the young man, "that matters are not so bad as you think. See, here is more milk in the pitcher."

So saying, he filled not only his own cup but also his companion's from the pitcher that was supposed to be empty. The good woman could hardly believe her eyes, for she had certainly poured out every drop in the pitcher.

"Wonder of wonders!" whispered good Baucis. "Did you ever see anything so strange?"

"Wife," answered Philemon, amazed and trembling, "I begin to think these are no common men. They must be mighty beings come from Mount Olympus!"

Then both fell upon their knees and begged pardon for the coarseness of the food and the rudeness of the table and the dishes. "They are the best that we have," they said. "Gladly would we give you something better, but we cannot."

The older traveler, who was none other than great Jupiter, raised them to their feet and smiled upon them. "The richest man in all the land could not have done more than you have done for our comfort," said he.

---

coarseness: commonness; inferior quality
rudeness: roughness

"Who are you, wonder-working strangers?" said Philemon in an awed whisper.

"We are your guests and your friends," replied the younger traveler, who was the god Mercury. With Jupiter, he had been traveling through that country to see how the people lived and whether they were kind-hearted and brave and true as all people ought to be. With a smile, he said to the old couple, "May your pitcher never be empty for your kind selves or the needy stranger!"

Then in grave, deep tones, Jupiter said, "But what shall we say for the people of the village who drove us from their doors and refused to give us shelter for the night?"

"I beg that you will not be too harsh with them," said Philemon. "They did not know who it was whom they treated so rudely."

"Nay," said Jupiter, "when men do not look upon the humblest stranger as if he were a brother, they are unworthy to walk the face of the earth."

"Ah me!" exclaimed Philemon. "If our neighbors knew what a blessed thing it is to be kind to strangers, they would tie up their dogs and not allow their children to fling stones."

"It is a sin and a shame for them to behave so," cried old Baucis. "I have a good mind to go the village this very day and tell them to mend their ways!"

"My dear old people," said the young man, "where is this village you talk about?" Then, with Jupiter, he led the old couple to the top of a nearby hill.

When they had reached the top of the steep slope, Mercury bade them look around. To their great wonder they saw that the village had disappeared and that a broad lake

bade: ordered

had taken its place. No house had been left standing save their own humble cottage.

"My good friends," said Jupiter, "you shall be rewarded for your hospitality. Is there not some favor that we can grant you?"

Then Philemon and Baucis both answered, "Let us finish our lives here where we have lived so long, and when the time comes for us to die, let us both pass from life together."

"You shall have your wish," said Jupiter.

Even while he spoke Philemon and Baucis saw a wonderful change come over their humble dwelling. Lofty columns took the place of the corner posts, the thatch was changed to a gilded roof, and the doors were hung with ornaments of gold. The cottage was transformed into a beautiful temple.

For many years the two old people were the keepers of the temple. But one day, as they were standing outside and looking up into the sky, they felt themselves stiffen so they could not stir. They had hardly time to say, "Good-bye, dear Philemon," and "Good-bye, dear Baucis," when they were changed into two noble trees—he into an oak and she into a linden.

And oh, what a pleasant shade they flung around them. Whenever a weary traveler paused under the trees, he seemed to hear the leaves whisper, "Welcome, dear traveler, welcome."

Long, long ago the temple fell in ruins and was forgotten, but the trees still stand side by side on the slope of the hill. When the wind rises, the people who pass that way hear the rustle of the leaves and see the branches caress each other, and they fancy that they hear the trees saying, "Dear Baucis!" — "Dear Philemon!"

---

gilded: covered with a thin layer of gold

HOW DO I LOVE THEE?
(SONNET 43)
by Elizabeth Barrett Browning

How do I love thee? Let me count the ways.
I love thee to the depth and breadth and height
My soul can reach, when feeling out of sight
For the ends of Being and ideal Grace.
I love thee to the level of everyday's
Most quiet need, by sun and candlelight.
I love thee freely, as men might strive for Right;
I love thee purely, as they turn from Praise.
I love thee with the passion put to use
In my old griefs, and with my childhood's faith.
I love thee with a love I seemed to lose
With my lost saints,—I love thee with the breath,
Smiles, tears, of all my life!—and, if God choose,
I shall but love thee better after death.

---

thee: you
breadth: width
being: existence
grace: goodness; mercy
strive: struggle; make a strong effort
passion: deep, strong emotion

ORPHEUS AND EURYDICE

Many were the minstrels who, in the early days of the world, went amongst men, telling them stories of the gods, of their wars and their births, and of the beginning of things. Of all these minstrels none was so famous as Orpheus; none could tell truer things about the gods. He himself was half divine, and there were some who said that he was in truth Apollo's son.

---

minstrels: in ancient times, singers of verses, often about heroes and
   their deeds
divine: from or of the gods

But a great grief came to Orpheus, a grief that stopped his singing and his playing upon the lyre. His young wife, Eurydice, was taken from him. One day, walking in the garden, she was bitten on the heel by a serpent; straightway she went down to the World of the Dead.

Then everything in this world was dark and bitter for the minstrel of the gods; sleep would not come to him, and for him food had no taste. Then Orpheus said, "I will do that which no mortal has ever done before; I will do that which even the Immortals might shrink from doing; I will go down into the World of the Dead, and I will bring back to the living and to the light my bride, Eurydice."

Then Orpheus went on his way to the cavern that goes down, down to the World of the Dead—the Cavern Tainaron. The trees showed him the way. As he went on, Orpheus played upon his lyre and sang; the trees heard his song and were moved by his grief, and with their arms and their heads they showed him the way to the deep, deep cavern named Tainaron.

Down, down, down by a winding path Orpheus went. He came at last to the great gate that opens upon the World of the Dead. And the silent guards who keep watch there for the Rulers of the Dead were astonished when they saw a living being coming towards them, and they would not let Orpheus approach the gate.

The minstrel took the lyre in his hands and played upon it. As he played, the silent watchers gathered around him, leaving the gate unguarded. As he played, the Rulers of the Dead came forth, Hades and Persephone, and listened to the words of the living man.

---

lyre: a musical instrument like a small harp
straightway: right away; immediately

"The cause of my coming through the dark and fearful ways," sang Orpheus, "is to strive to gain a fairer fate for Eurydice, my bride. All that is above must come down to you at last, O Rulers of the most lasting World. But before her time has Eurydice been brought here. I have desired strength to endure her loss, but I cannot endure it. And I have come before you, Hades and Persephone, brought here by love."

When Orpheus said the name of love, Persephone, the queen of the dead, bowed her young head, and bearded Hades, the king, bowed his head also. Persephone remembered how Demeter, her mother, had sought her all through the world, and she remembered the touch of her mother's tears upon her face. And Hades remembered how his love for Persephone had led him to carry her away from the valley where she had been gathering flowers. He and Persephone stood aside, and Orpheus went through the gate and came amongst the dead.

Still upon his lyre he played. Tantalus—who for his crime had been condemned to stand up to his neck in water and yet never be able to quench his thirst—Tantalus heard, and for a while did not strive to put his lips toward the water that ever flowed away from him; Sisyphus—who had been condemned to roll up a hill a stone that ever rolled back—Sisyphus heard the music that Orpheus played, and for a while he sat still upon his stone. Ixion, bound to a wheel, stopped its turning for a while; the vultures abandoned their torment of Tityos; the daughters of Danaos ceased to fill their jars; even those dread ones, the Erinyes, who bring to the dead the memories of all their crimes and all their faults, had their cheeks wet with tears.

---

endure: to stand; to bear
condemned: sentenced; doomed
quench: to satisfy

In the throng of the newly-come dead, Orpheus saw Eurydice. She looked upon her husband, but she had not the power to come near him. But slowly she came when Hades called her. Then with joy Orpheus took her hands.

It would be granted them—no mortal ever gained such privilege before— to leave, both together, the World of the Dead, and to abide for another space in the World of the Living. One condition there would be—that on their way up neither Orpheus nor Eurydice should look back.

They went through the gate and came out amongst the watchers that are around the portals. These showed them the path that went up to the World of the Living. That way they went, Orpheus and Eurydice, he going before her.

Up and through the darkened ways they went, Orpheus knowing that Eurydice was behind him, but never looking back upon her. As he went, his heart was filled with things to tell her—how the trees were blossoming in the garden she had left; how the water was sparkling in the fountain; how the doors of the house stood open; how they, sitting together, would watch the sunlight on the laurel bushes. All these things were in his heart to tell her who came behind him, silent and unseen.

And now they were nearing the place where the cavern opened on the World of the Living. Orpheus looked up toward the light from the sky. Out of the opening of the cavern he went; he saw a white-winged bird fly by. He turned around and cried, "O, Eurydice, look upon the world I have won you back to!"

He turned to say this to her. He saw her with her long dark hair and pale face. He held out his arms to clasp her.

---

abide: to stay in a place
portals: doors

But in that instant she slipped back into the gloom of the cavern. And all he heard spoken was a single word, "Farewell!" Long, long had it taken Eurydice to climb so far, but in the moment of his turning around she had fallen back to her place amongst the dead. For Orpheus had looked back.

Back through the cavern Orpheus went again. Again he came before the watchers of the gate. But now he was not looked at nor listened to; hopeless, he had to return to the World of the Living.

DAMON AND PYTHIAS

dramatized for radio by Fan Kissen

Cast

DAMON	**PYTHIAS**	**KING**
FIRST VOICE	**SECOND VOICE**	**THIRD VOICE**
FIRST ROBBER	**SECOND ROBBER**	**SOLDIER**
MOTHER	**NARRATOR**	

(Sound: Iron door opens and shuts. Key in lock.)
(Music: Up full and out.)

NARRATOR: Long, long ago there lived on the island of Sicily two young men named Damon and Pythias. They were known far and wide for the strong friendship each had for the other. Their names have come down to our own times to mean true friendship. You may hear it said of two persons:

FIRST VOICE: Those two? Why, they're like Damon and Pythias!

NARRATOR: The king of that country was a cruel tyrant. He made cruel laws, and he showed no mercy toward anyone who broke his laws. Now, you might very well wonder:

SECOND VOICE: Why didn't the people rebel?

NARRATOR: Well, the people didn't dare rebel because they feared the king's great and powerful army. No one dared say a word against the king or his laws—except Damon and Pythias speaking against a new law the king had proclaimed.

---

tyrant: a ruler who uses power cruelly and unjustly

SOLDIER: Ho, there! Who are you that dares to speak so about our king?

PYTHIAS: *(Unafraid)* I am called Pythias.

SOLDIER: Don't you know it is a crime to speak against the king or his laws? You are under arrest! Come and tell this opinion of yours to the king's face!

(Music: A few short bars in and out.)

NARRATOR: When Pythias was brought before the king, he showed no fear. He stood straight and quiet before the throne.

KING: *(Hard, cruel)* So, Pythias! They tell me you do not approve of the laws I make.

PYTHIAS: I am not alone, your majesty, in thinking your laws are cruel. But you rule the people with such an iron hand that they dare not complain.

KING: *(Angry)* But you have the daring to complain for them! Have they appointed you their champion?

PYTHIAS: No, your majesty. I speak for myself alone. I have no wish to make trouble for anyone. But I am not afraid to tell you that the people are suffering under your rule. They want to have a voice in making the laws for themselves. You do not allow them to speak up for themselves.

KING: In other words, you are calling me a tyrant! Well, you shall learn for yourself how a tyrant treats a rebel! Soldier! Throw this man into prison!

SOLDIER: At once, your majesty! Don't try to resist, Pythias!

PYTHIAS: I know better than to try to resist a soldier of the king! And for how long am I to remain in prison, your majesty, merely for speaking out for the people?

KING: *(Cruel)* Not for very long, Pythias. Two weeks from today at noon, you shall be put to death in the public square as an example to anyone else who may dare to question my laws or acts. Off to prison with him, soldier!

(Music: In briefly and out.)

NARRATOR: When Damon heard that his friend Pythias had been thrown into prison, and about the severe punishment that was to follow, he was heartbroken. He rushed to the prison and persuaded the guard to let him speak to his friend.

DAMON: Oh, Pythias! How terrible to find you here! I wish I could do something to save you!

PYTHIAS: Nothing can save me, Damon, my dear friend. I am prepared to die. But there is one thought that troubles me greatly.

DAMON: What is it? I will do anything to help you.

PYTHIAS: I'm worried about what will happen to my mother and my sister when I'm gone.

DAMON: I'll take care of them, Pythias, as if they were my own mother and sister.

PYTHIAS: Thank you, Damon. I have money to leave them. But there are other things I must arrange. If only I could go see them before I die! But they live two days' journey from here, you know.

DAMON: I'll go to the king and beg him to give you your freedom for a few days. You'll give your word to return at the end of that time. Everyone in Sicily knows you for a man who has never broken his word.

PYTHIAS: Do you believe for one moment that the king would let me leave this prison, no matter how good my word may have been all my life?

DAMON: I'll tell him that I shall take your place in the prison cell. I'll tell him that if you do not return by the appointed day, he may kill me in your place!

PYTHIAS: No, no, Damon! You must not do such a foolish thing! I cannot—I will not—let you do this! Damon! Damon! Don't go! *(To himself)* Damon, my friend! You may find yourself in a cell beside me!

(Music: In briefly and out.)

DAMON: *(Begging)* Your majesty! I beg of you! Let Pythias go home for a few days to bid farewell to his mother and sister. He gives his word that he will return at your appointed time. Everyone knows that his word can be trusted.

KING: In ordinary business affairs—perhaps. But he is now a man under sentence of death. To free him even for a few days would strain his honesty—any man's honesty—too far. Pythias would never return here! I consider him a traitor, but I'm certain he's no fool.

DAMON: Your majesty! I will take his place in the prison until he comes back. If he does not return, then you may take my life in his place.

KING: *(Astonished)* What did you say, Damon?

DAMON: I'm so certain of Pythias that I am offering to die in his place if he fails to return on time.

KING: I can't believe you mean it!

DAMON: I do mean it, your majesty.

KING: You make me very curious, Damon, so curious that I'm willing to put you and Pythias to the test. This exchange of prisoners will be made. But Pythias must be back two weeks from today, at noon.

DAMON: Thank you, your majesty!

KING: The order with my official seal shall go by your own hand, Damon. But I warn you, if your friend does not return on time, you shall surely die in his place! I shall show no mercy.

---

traitor: a person who betrays a cause or country

(Music: In briefly and out.)

NARRATOR: Pythias did not like the king's bargain with Damon. He did not like to leave his friend in prison with the chance that he might lose his life if something went wrong. But at last Damon persuaded him to leave and Pythias set out for his home. More than a week went by. The day set for the death sentence drew near. Pythias did not return.

Everyone in the city knew of the condition on which the king had permitted Pythias to go home. Everywhere people met, the talk was sure to turn to the two friends.

FIRST VOICE: Do you suppose Pythias will come back?

SECOND VOICE: Why should he stick his head under the king's ax once he has escaped?

THIRD VOICE: Still, would an honorable man like Pythias let such a good friend die for him?

FIRST VOICE: There's no telling what a man will do when it's a question of his own life against another's.

SECOND VOICE: But if Pythias doesn't come back before the time is up, he will be killing his friend.

THIRD VOICE: Well, there's still a few days' time. I, for one, am certain that Pythias will return in time.

SECOND VOICE: And I am just as certain that he will not. Friendship is friendship, but a man's own life is something stronger, I say!

NARRATOR: Two days before the time was up, the king himself visited Damon in his prison cell.

(Sound: Iron door unlocked and opened)

KING: *(Mocking)* You see now, Damon, that you were a fool to make this bargain. Your friend has tricked you! He will not come back here to be killed! He has deserted you.

---

deserted: left behind; abandoned

DAMON: *(Calm and firm)* I have faith in my friend. I know he will return.

KING: *(Mocking)* We shall see!

(Sound: Iron door shut and locked.)

NARRATOR: Meanwhile, when Pythias reached the home of his family, he arranged his business affairs so that his mother and sister would be able to live comfortably for the rest of their years. Then he said a last farewell to them before starting back to the city.

MOTHER: *(In tears)* Pythias, it will take you two days to get back. Stay another day, I beg you!

PYTHIAS: I dare not stay longer, Mother. Remember, Damon is locked up in my prison cell while I'm gone. Please don't weep for me. My death may help bring better days for all our people.

NARRATOR: So Pythias began his journey in plenty of time. But bad luck struck him on the very first day. At twilight, as he walked along a lonely stretch of woodland, a rough voice called:

FIRST ROBBER: Not so fast there, young man! Stop!

PYTHIAS: *(Startled)* Oh! What is it? What do you want?

SECOND ROBBER: Your money bags.

PYTHIAS: My money bags? I have only this small bag of coins. I shall need them for some favors, perhaps, before I die.

FIRST ROBBER: What do you mean, before you die? We don't mean to kill you, only take your money.

PYTHIAS: I'll give you my money, only don't delay me any longer. I am to die by the king's order three days from now. If I don't return on time, my friend must die in my place.

FIRST ROBBER: A likely story! What man would be fool enough to go back to prison ready to die?

SECOND ROBBER: And what man would be fool enough to die for you?

FIRST ROBBER: We'll take your money, all right. And we'll tie you up while we get away.

PYTHIAS: *(Begging)* No! No! I must get back to free my friend! *(Fade)* I must go back!

NARRATOR: But the two robbers took Pythias's money, tied him to a tree, and went off as fast as they could. Pythias struggled to free himself. He cried out for a long time. But no one traveled through that lonesome woodland after dark. The sun had been up for many hours before he finally managed to free himself from the ropes that had tied him to the tree. He lay on the ground, hardly able to breathe.

(Music: In briefly and out.)

NARRATOR: After a while Pythias got to his feet. Weak and dizzy from hunger and thirst and his struggle to free himself, he set off again. Day and night he traveled without stopping, desperately trying to reach the city in time to save Damon's life.

(Music: Up and out.)

NARRATOR: On the last day, half an hour before noon, Damon's hands were tied behind his back, and he was taken into the public square. The people muttered angrily as Damon was led in by the jailer. Then the king entered and seated himself on a high platform.

(Sound: Crowd voices in and hold under single voices.)

SOLDIER: *(Loud)* Long live the king!

FIRST VOICE: *(Low)* The longer he lives, the more miserable our lives will be!

KING: *(Loud, mocking)* Well, Damon, your lifetime is nearly up. Where is your good friend Pythias now?

DAMON: *(Firm)* I have faith in my friend. If he has not returned, I'm certain it is through no fault of his own.

KING: *(Mocking)* The sun is almost overhead. The shadow is almost at the noon mark. And still your friend has not returned to give back your life!

DAMON: *(Quiet)* I am ready and happy to die in his place.

KING: *(Harsh)* And you shall, Damon! Jailer, lead the prisoner to the—

(Sound: Crowd voices up to a roar, then under.)

FIRST VOICE: *(Over noise)* Look! It's Pythias!

SECOND VOICE: *(Over noise)* Pythias has come back!

PYTHIAS: *(Breathless)* Let me through! Damon!

DAMON: Pythias!

PYTHIAS: Thank the gods I'm not too late!

DAMON: *(Quiet, sincere)* I would have died for you gladly, my friend.

CROWD VOICES: *(Loud, demanding)* Set them free! Set them both free!

KING: *(Loud)* People of the city! *(Crowd voices out.)* Never in all my life have I seen such faith and friendship, such loyalty between men. There are many among you who call me harsh and cruel. But I cannot kill any man who proves such strong and true friendship for another. Damon and Pythias, I set you both free. *(Roar of approval from crowd.)* I am king. I command a great army. I have stores of gold and precious jewels. But I would give all my money and power for one friend like Damon or Pythias.

(Sound: Roar of approval from crowd up briefly and out.)
(Music: Up and out.)

FRIENDSHIP

Friendship needs no studied phrases,
    Polished face, or winning wiles;
Friendship deals no lavish praises,
    Friendship dons no surface smiles.

Friendship follows Nature's diction,
    Shuns the blandishments of art,
Boldly severs truth from fiction,
    Speaks the language of the heart.

Friendship favors no condition,
    Scorns a narrow-minded creed,
Lovingly fulfills its mission,
    Be it word or be it deed.

Friendship cheers the faint and weary,
    Makes the timid spirit brave,
Warns the erring, lights the dreary,
    Smooths the passage to the grave.

Friendship—pure, unselfish friendship,
    All through life's allotted span,
Nurtures, strengthens, widens, lengthens,
    Man's relationship with man.

studied: carefully made	blandishments: flattery; false praise
wiles: tricks	severs: separates; cuts off
lavish: excessive	creed: a set of beliefs
dons: puts on	erring: those who make mistakes
diction: way of speaking; use of words	allotted: a given portion
shuns: rejects	nurtures: nourishes; develops

ECHO AND NARCISSUS

Among the trees of the forest, where the cool streams run, beautiful wood-nymphs used to have their homes. They loved to play in the flickering sunlight and under the dancing leaves, and people sometimes caught sight of the gleam of their white feet as they dipped them in the rushing waters of the brook.

There was one nymph named Echo, whose chief amusement was to tease and play tricks on her companions. "Daphne! Oh, come here! Quick—just see!" she would sometimes call. And when Daphne would come running to the spot, eager to see what there was to be seen, Echo would have vanished as completely as if she had never been there, until a stifled laugh soon revealed her hiding place.

Echo was a great chatterer; she never listened to anyone else, but was sure to talk a great deal herself. One day she came upon a shepherd sitting on a rock, watching his sheep as they cropped the grass below. She noticed that some of the sheep were beginning to stray from the flock. Thinking this a fine chance for a bit of fun, she at once began to laugh and talk with the shepherd. She so distracted him that soon not one of the flock was left in sight. And then, with a laugh at the dismayed face of the shepherd, Echo, too, ran away and left him.

---

gleam: glow
chief: main; most important
stifled: muffled; held back
cropped: bit off the upper parts
dismayed: discouraged; confused and saddened

At first the other nymphs used to laugh at her nonsense and enjoyed the fun as much as Echo herself did. But as she was continually playing tricks upon everybody, and as the tricks, like the trick she played on the shepherd, were often unkind ones, her companions gradually came to avoid her.

One day it happened that Juno, the queen of the gods, came to the forest. Echo troubled her so much with her foolish chattering that finally Juno turned upon the teasing nymph and declared in anger, "Enough! We are all weary of your nonsense. Your tongue is useless to us, so from this moment forth, it shall also be useless to you. Henceforth your speech shall be even shorter than your tongue. Never again will you start a conversation, nor may you even reply, unless it is to repeat what was spoken to you."

Echo, ashamed and sorry, went away into the deep woods. There she dwelt alone, until one afternoon, she spied a handsome youth, named Narcissus, as he wandered among the trees.

Narcissus was tall and lithe, with eyes like twin stars, a mouth like Cupid's bow, and flowing curls to rival Apollo's. Echo loved him at once and longed to call out to him, but by Juno's decree, she could not. So, instead, she followed him as he made his way through the forest, and waited for him to speak.

At last, Narcissus heard a branch break under her foot and cried out, "Who is here?"

---

henceforth: from this time forward
lithe: slim, graceful, and athletic
rival: to compete with; to strive to be better than
decree: command; official order

Echo answered, "Here!"

Narcissus looked around, but saw no one. "Come here!" he called impatiently.

"Come here!" came Echo's reply.

Again, Narcissus turned around and peered among the trees, but still he saw no one. Frustrated, he cried, "Speak, and step forth!"

"Step forth!" answered Echo, and impulsively she dashed from the trees and flung her arms around his neck.

"Take your hands off me!" shouted Narcissus, jumping back. "I will die before I love thee!"

"I love thee!" Echo sobbed.

But Narcissus hurried away, and Echo fled far into the woods, there to bury her blushing face in the green leaves. Heartbroken, she hid in the mountain caves and cliffs, and pined for Narcissus until sorrow bore away her body, leaving only her voice behind. Still she is ready to reply to anyone who calls her: If the call is a laughing one, she laughs back; if it is sad, she answers mournfully.

As for Narcissus, he shunned all the rest of the nymphs as he had done poor Echo. Then one day, a maiden who had long tried to attract him, but in vain, uttered a prayer that he might feel what it was to love but receive no love in return. The avenging goddess, Nemesis, heard and granted the prayer.

Deep in the wood, there was a clear fountain, with water like silver, to which the shepherds never drove their flocks. Wild beasts had not disturbed it, nor had branch or leaf fallen

---

impulsively: without thinking ahead

shunned: avoided on purpose

in vain: without success

avenging: taking revenge for; getting even for some injury or insult

into its calm waters, but the grass grew fresh around it, and the rocks sheltered it from the sun. Hither came the youth, fatigued with hunting, heated and thirsty. He stooped down to drink, and saw his own image in the water. He thought it was some beautiful water spirit living in the fountain. He stood gazing with admiration at those bright eyes, those locks curled like the locks of Apollo, the ivory neck, the parted lips, and the glow of health over all. He fell in love with his own image.

He smiled, and the image smiled back. He reached out, and the image seemed to reach back. Then he thrust his arms into the water to fling his arms around it, but the motion disturbed the water and caused the image to disappear.

"Why did you leave me?" cried Narcissus to his reflection. "When I smiled, you smiled, and when I reached out to you, you reached back to me. But when I tried to clasp you in my arms, you fled!"

Thus Narcissus mourned, but the image did not answer him. Yet he could not tear himself away. He lost all thought of food or rest, while he hovered over the brink of the fountain gazing upon his own image. And as fire melts wax or the heat of the sun burns away frost, so did grief waste away Narcissus.

In time, Echo finally found him, with his strength, vigor, and handsome form all but gone. Though he had scorned her, she only pitied him. As often as he sighed, "Alas! Alas!" she softly answered, "Alas!" And when with his last breath

hither: here
fatigued: worn out; exhausted
hovered: stayed suspended above something else
vigor: energy; strength of mind or body

he looked into the water and sighed, "Ah, my beloved, farewell!" Echo sighed, "Beloved, farewell!"

The water-nymphs wept for Narcissus, and Echo resounded their mourning. But when they looked for his body, it had vanished. In its place by the edge of the spring there had grown up a little flower, golden within, and surrounded with white leaves, which bears the name and preserves the memory of Narcissus.

resounded: echoed
preserves: keeps alive; maintains

CUPID AND PSYCHE

There was once a king who had two lovely daughters. The elder was as fair as a summer's day, and the younger glowed like an autumn sunset. But then a third daughter was born to the king, and this girl was the most beautiful maiden the world had ever seen. She was called Psyche, a name that means "the Soul."

Whenever Psyche traveled through the city, the people lined the streets to watch her and marvel at her beauty. Strangers from every corner of the kingdom and from distant countries braved dangerous journeys over land and sea just to catch a glimpse of her.

"She is as beautiful as Venus herself," some cried, strewing flowers in her path.

"She is even more glorious than Venus," answered others, "for she is here and Venus is far away on Mount Olympus."

So they left Venus's temples untended, and sang their songs of praise and honor to Psyche instead.

Such doings did not escape Venus's notice. "Imagine!" cried the goddess of love. "They love Psyche because of me, yet they have spurned me because of her. I will punish her, and bring shame upon them all!"

Then Venus called out to her son, whom she called Cupid, but whom others knew simply by the name of Love. "Come,"

---

marvel: to wonder at; to be filled with astonishment
untended: uncared for; ignored
spurned: rejected scornfully

she cried, "and avenge this insult to your mother. Bring your bow, and bring your arrows, which neither gods nor men can resist. Use your power to make Psyche fall in love with the most miserable, vile, and wretched creature alive."

Cupid prepared his golden arrows, and when the stars came out, he flew down into Psyche's chamber. But when he saw the sleeping princess, it was as if he had pierced his heart with one of his own arrows, for he too fell deeply in love with the girl.

Sighing, he hung his bow on his shoulder, returned his arrows to their quiver, and raced home to Mount Olympus. He never whispered a word of what had happened, for he knew his mother would be furious if she found out that he had fallen in love with Psyche.

Long and eagerly did Venus wait, but never did Psyche fall in love with any vile creature. Still, to keep the girl from happiness, the goddess made it so that even though men looked upon Psyche with wonder and awe, no man would fall in love with her. Even though both her sisters had been married to kings, no man—be he king, prince, or peasant— sought Psyche's hand in marriage.

At last, the king and queen grew dismayed that their lovely daughter was not wed, and decided to ask an oracle how they might find a husband for her. The oracle replied, "Psyche shall never wed a mortal man. She shall be given to the one who waits for her on yonder mountain—a winged creature who overcomes gods and men."

"A monster?" they cried, and wept because the oracle would say no more.

---

avenge: to get revenge for; to get even for
vile: foul; repulsive; horrible
oracle: in mythology, a being who was believed to have knowledge from the gods
yonder: over there in the distance

But when they told the news to Psyche, she said sternly, "Why do you weep? You should have wept when the people honored me and called me as beautiful as Venus. Now she is angry, and there is only one way to appease her. Bring me to the mountain, and leave me for the monster."

The king and queen argued and pleaded with her, but Psyche would not change her mind. So, at last, together with a great company of mourners, they led the princess to the mountain, to be an offering to the monster of whom the oracle had spoken.

All alone, Psyche watched her parents and her people walk slowly down the mountain path. Only when they disappeared from sight did she begin to weep. But then a sudden breeze drew near, dried her tears, and caressed her hair, seeming to murmur comfort. It was Zephyr, the kindly West Wind, come to befriend her. Psyche took heart, and the gentle wind lifted her in his arms, and bore her on strong wings over the mountain, into the valley below. He laid her on a bed of soft grass, and there the princess fell asleep.

When Psyche awoke, she saw that she lay at the edge of a forest, with a river as clear as crystal running by her feet. Making her way among the mighty trees, she followed the river deeper and deeper into the woods, until she came to a great clearing, where stood a shining palace with pillars of gold and walls of silver. A path made of precious stones led to the gleaming front doors, which were flung wide open to the world.

Shyly, Psyche entered the palace, and stood wondering at its richness. As she gazed, soft airs stirred about her, and, little by little, the silence was filled with gentle murmurs. One voice, sweeter than the rest, whispered, "All that you see

appease: to calm; to make peaceful

is yours, dear Psyche. Fear nothing; only command us, for we are here to serve you."

Astonished and delighted, Psyche followed the voice from hall to hall, each room full to bursting with everything that could delight a young princess. There was even a sunlit pool, brightly tiled and fed with running waters, where she bathed her weary limbs. And after she had put on the fine new clothes that lay ready for her, a long table crowded with delicious dishes appeared, and a chair was pulled up for her beside it.

The moment Psyche sat down, a host of invisible servants brought forth a parade of bread, fruit, sweets, and cider. An invisible bard told stories, and a troupe of invisible musicians played soothing music.

Finally, when night fell and all the palace was dark, Cupid himself flew down from the heavens. The gleaming palace doors opened for him, for he was the lord of the palace, and he wished Psyche to be its lady. Against his mother's command, he wished to marry Psyche, and that very evening, under cover of darkness, he spoke so kindly to her that, though she saw him not, she fell in love and agreed to be his wife.

Just before the first rays of dawn, Cupid flew from Psyche's side. And so it went on—at night he came to her, but always he left before dawn, and did not return until darkness fell again. And though she begged him to stay and asked to see his face, he always refused.

"Never doubt me, dearest Psyche," said he. "Perhaps you would fear if you saw me, and love is all I ask. There is a reason why I must be hidden now. Only believe me."

---

limbs: arms and legs
host: a very large number
bard: a poet who sang tales of heroic deeds

For many days Psyche was content. But when she grew used to happiness, she thought once more of her parents mourning her as lost, and of her sisters, with whom she wished to share her new joy and treasures. One night she told her husband of her wish, and begged that her sisters at least might come to see her. He sighed, but did not refuse.

"Zephyr shall bring them here," he said. And the next morning, swift as a bird, the West Wind came over the crest of the high mountain and down into the enchanted valley, bearing her two sisters.

They greeted Psyche with tears of joy, amazed to find her still alive. But when Psyche led them through her palace and showed them all her treasures, envy took root in their hearts. While they feasted with her, they grew more and more bitter. Hoping to find some flaw in her good fortune, they asked a thousand questions.

"Where is your husband?" they asked. "And why is he not here with you?"

"He is—he is gone," stammered Psyche. "All day, he will be hunting in the mountains."

"What does he look like?" they asked.

"He is young and handsome," said Psyche. But when the sisters pressed her to tell more, she could find no answer.

"Why, sister," they cried, "have you truly seen this husband of yours? Or are you walking in a dream—or worse, a nightmare? Wake, before it is too late! Have you forgotten what the oracle declared, that you were destined for a monster, the fear of gods and men? Are you deceived by his show of kindness?"

---

destined: fated; determined beforehand
deceived: fooled; tricked

Psyche trembled but would say no word against her husband.

"We have come to warn you," the jealous sisters continued. "The people told us, as we came over the mountain, that your husband is a terrible dragon. He feeds you well now only because he wishes to devour you later. Tonight, you must take a dagger, and when the monster is asleep, go, light a lamp, and look at him. You can kill him easily, and all his riches will be yours—and ours."

Psyche was horrified by her sisters' wicked plan. Nevertheless, after they left, she brooded over what they had said. She did not see that they were lying and wished her ill. Instead, suspicion ate like a moth into her lovely mind, and by nightfall, she had hidden a lamp and a dagger in her chamber.

Toward midnight, when her husband was fast asleep, Psyche rose, lit the lamp, and drew out the dagger. Hardly daring to breathe, she went softly to his side, and shone the light on him, fearing to see a monster.

There in the glow, the youngest of the gods lay sleeping, the most beautiful, most irresistible of all immortals. His hair shone golden as the sun, his face was as radiant as spring, and from his shoulders sprang two white wings. Psyche gasped and leaned closer to him, filled with awe. But her hands trembled, and some burning oil from the lamp fell on his shoulder and burned him.

Cupid's eyes opened. At once he saw his wife—and the dark suspicion in her heart.

---

devour: to eat greedily
brooded: worried; thought gloomily
radiant: bright and shining

"O doubting Psyche!" he wailed. "Where there is no trust, Love cannot stay." Then he flew out the window and disappeared into the night like a shooting star.

Wild with sorrow, Psyche tried to follow him. "Love was my husband," she wailed, "but I have lost him." Then she fell senseless to the ground. When she came to, she looked all around. She was alone, and the place was beautiful no longer. Garden and palace had vanished with Love.

"Perhaps I have lost Love forever," said Psyche, "but I will seek him everywhere, and if I find him, perhaps he will forgive me."

Psyche wandered for months, over mountains and through valleys, across vast plains and rushing rivers, but she did not find Love. She visited the temples of the gods and goddesses, but none would help her, for fear of bringing Venus's anger upon themselves. So she called up her courage, went to the house of Venus, and offered to serve the Queen of Love herself.

"Foolish girl," snapped Venus. "Do you think you can make amends for the wound you gave your husband? I will certainly see that you do. There is always work for people as clever as you."

She led Psyche into a great chamber heaped high with mingled wheat, barley, millet, lentils, and beans. "Separate these grains by nightfall," commanded Venus as she whirled out the door, "or else I will banish you and make you wander forever!"

Tears filled Psyche's eyes as she looked at the mountain of grain. What good was it to begin an impossible task? Then

---

make amends: to make up for some loss, injury, or mistake
mingled: mixed
banish: to send away and forbid to return

she noticed a moving thread of black pouring out from a crack in the wall. It was a long line of ants. These tiny creatures had taken pity on the girl whom the gods had forsaken. The ants worked so swiftly and diligently that all the grains were separated into neat piles long before the sun sank beneath the horizon.

When Venus returned, she was furious to see the task completed. "Deceitful girl," she shrieked, "this is not your work. But it does not matter. Tomorrow's task will require more wit than you have in your dull head." Then she threw a crust of black bread at Psyche and stormed out of the chamber.

In the morning, Venus led Psyche to the bank of a wide river. Pointing to the land across the water, she said, "Go now to yonder grove where the sheep with the golden fleece are grazing. Bring me a golden lock from every one of them, or else I will banish you and make you wander forever."

Psyche bade the goddess farewell and began to cross the river. But as Venus disappeared, the river-reeds bent toward her and sang, "Have a care, Psyche. This flock has not the gentle ways of sheep. While the sun is high, they are as fierce as flame. But when the shadows are long, they go to sleep under the trees. While they sleep, you may cross the river without fear and pick the golden fleece off the thorn-bushes in the pasture."

Thanking the reeds, Psyche sat down to rest beside them. When the sheep began to doze in the shadows of the trees, Psyche crossed the river and pulled the tufts of golden fleece off the thorn-bushes. By twilight, she returned to Venus with her arms full of shining fleece.

---

forsaken: turned away from; abandoned
deceitful: tending to cheat, trick, or lie to others
bade: told

"Someone helped you," raged Venus. "Let us see, though, who will help you with this. Go now, with this little box, down to Proserpina in Hades and ask her to enclose in it some of her beauty, for I have grown pale in caring for my wounded son."

Psyche shuddered, for she knew that if she failed, she would never leave the Land of the Dead. Still, she went forth, hoping and yet fearing to find the dark road to the underworld. Just as she was beginning to despair, a friendly voice from a nearby tower said to her, "Stay, Psyche, I know your grief. Only listen, and I will tell you a safe way through all these trials." And the voice went on to tell her how she could avoid all the dangers of Hades and return unharmed.

"Above all," added the voice, "when Proserpina has returned the box, do not open it. It is not wise to be too curious about divine beauty."

Psyche thanked the voice, and followed its instructions. She found her way safely into Hades, received the box of beauty from Proserpina, and was soon in the upper world again, weary but hopeful.

"Surely Love has not forgotten me," she said. "But humbled as I am and worn with toil, how shall I ever please him? Venus does not need all of the beauty in this casket. And since I am using it for Love's sake, it must be right to take some."

So she reasoned with herself. She opened the box. But the gifts of Hades and Proserpina are not for mortal maids. A strange smoke curled up from the box, causing Psyche to fall down like one dead, overcome with sleep.

In the meantime, Cupid's wound had healed. Though Venus had locked him in his chamber to keep him from Psyche, it is

despair: to lose hope

no easy task to keep Love imprisoned. Indeed, he managed to escape, and his first thought was to seek out his wife.

When he found Psyche, with one pass of his hand he wiped the sleep away from her eyes and mind, and put it back into the box. Then he pricked her gently with one of his arrows and said, "O doubting Psyche! Again your curiosity has almost cost you everything. But go now and finish your errand, and I will take care of all the rest."

Psyche returned to Venus's palace with a light heart and gave her the box, while Cupid hastened to Mount Olympus, where all the gods sat feasting in Jupiter's hall.

"Oh ye gods," cried Cupid, "Love has found his love. But my mother is angry and jealous and resists my wishes."

Jupiter smiled. "Who can resist Love?" he chuckled. "We will bring Psyche here and welcome her among us." And he himself coaxed Venus with kind words until at last she relented and blessed the marriage.

When Psyche arrived at the great feast, Jupiter gave her ambrosia to eat and nectar to drink. As the sweet liquid ran down her throat, light came to her face like moonrise, and Psyche blossomed into immortality.

And so at last, after many trials, Cupid and Psyche—or, as one might also say, Love and the Soul—were united, never to be parted again.

---

coaxed: persuaded with kind words and flattery
relented: gave in
ambrosia: in Greek and Roman mythology, the food of the gods

Pygmalion and Galatea

Once, on the island of Cyprus, there lived a sculptor whose heart was as hard and cold as the stone he carved. This sculptor, called Pygmalion, lived only for his art. He thought nothing as good or as beautiful as the white marble folk that live without faults and never grow old. He disdained to marry a mortal woman, for all seemed to him full of imperfections compared to his flawless sculptures. And so he lived alone among his statues.

But it happened one day that he came across a block of pure white marble, and the spark of an idea caught in his mind. He took the block home with him, and began to carve from it a statue of a maiden. By evening, tender fingers seemed to reach out to him from the marble, and at sight of them, Pygmalion began to carve as though the steeds of Helios were breathing their fiery smoke at his back. He worked tirelessly, day and night, drawing out the statue's graceful figure, giving her all the beauty of his dreams.

Then Pygmalion rested from his efforts and gazed upon the statue—if, indeed, statue it was. For such was his skill that the figure before him seemed more a creature of living, breathing flesh and blood rather than cold marble. With both hands, he caressed her face in wonder. Then no longer thinking of her as a statue, but as the dear companion of his life, he kissed her, for Pygmalion had fallen in love with his creation.

---

disdained: scorned; refused contemptuously
flawless: perfect; without any mistake or defect
caressed: touched gently and with affection

He named the statue Galatea, and, like a child with a toy, he pretended she was real. He arrayed her like a princess, draping her in fine clothing and jewelry. He brought her sweetly singing birds and fragrant flowers of a thousand colors, pretending such gifts would please her. At night he tucked her into bed, as little girls do with their favorite dolls, and sang gently, believing she might be comforted.

But in his heart, Pygmalion was miserable, because of course Galatea did not return his affection. In the end, all his pretending led to sorrow, and her cold, lifeless perfection became a torment to him.

About that time, the people of Cyprus began to prepare for the festival of Venus. There they kept her temples with such honor that it was said that if any person on the island called upon the goddess, she would listen.

On the day of the festival, thousands of people flocked to the temples, made offerings, and asked Venus to grant their wishes that, whomever they loved, their love might be returned. As the day drew to a close, Pygmalion, too, approached the altar and made his offering to the Queen of Love. "If it is true that you can give all things," he said, "I pray to have as my wife"—but he did not dare to say, "my statue-maiden," so instead, he muttered, "a woman like my statue-maiden."

Venus heard, and she knew exactly what he meant.

Meanwhile, the sculptor hurried home, unwilling to be parted even for a day from his love. There she stood, as always, upon her pedestal.

But when he looked at her, it seemed as though the sunset had shed a flush of life upon her marble skin. Pygmalion

---

arrayed: dressed in an impressive way
torment: extreme pain of the body or mind

drew near in wonder, and felt, instead of the chill air of hard stone, a gentle warmth around her, soft as a baby's breath. He touched her hand, and her marble skin yielded to his touch, softening like wax in the sun. He held her wrist, and felt a heartbeat pulsing in her veins.

Then, pouring out his thanks to Venus, Pygmalion kissed Galatea. The maiden's face bloomed like a waking rose. She opened her eyes, smiled, and stepped down from her pedestal to stand beside him—for the hearts of both the man and the maiden had come alive at last.

And it is said that Venus herself graced their wedding, and blessed the love that had blossomed among the stones.

ACKNOWLEDGMENTS

Text

The Golden Age; The Story of Prometheus; The Story of Pandora; Perseus and the Quest for Medusa's Head; Atalanta, the Fleet-Footed Huntress; and The Adventures of Theseus adapted from *Old Greek Stories* by James Baldwin (New York: American Book Company, 1895)

Baucis and Philemon; The Story of Pandora [conclusion only] adapted from *A Wonder-Book for Girls and Boys* by Nathaniel Hawthorne (1852)

Jason and the Golden Fleece adapted from *The Greek Heroes* by Charles Kingsley (New York: Macmillan, 1894)

Orpheus and Eurydice adapted from *The Golden Fleece and the Heroes Who Lived Before Achilles* by Padraic Colum (New York: Macmillan, 1921)

"The Legend of Damon and Pythias" by Fan Kissen from THE BAG of FIRE AND OTHER PLAYS by Fan Kissen. Copyright © 1964 by Houghton Mifflin Company, copyright renewed © 1993 by John Kissen Heaslip. Reprinted by permission of Houghton Mifflin Company. All rights reserved.

Echo and Narcissus adapted from *The Age of Fable, or Beauties of Mythology* by Thomas Bulfinch (Boston: Lothrop, Lee, and Shepard, 1906)

Cupid and Psyche; Pygmalion and Galatea adapted from *Old Greek Folk Stories Told Anew* by Josephine Preston Peabody (Boston: Houghton Mifflin, 1897)

Illustrations

Seven illustrations by Steele Savage from MYTHOLOGY by Edith Hamilton. Copyright © 1942 by Edith Hamilton; Copyright © renewed 1969 by Dorian Fielding Reid and Doris Fielding Reid. By permission of Little, Brown, and Company, Inc.

Five illustrations by Steele Savage from STORIES OF GODS AND HEROES by Sally Benson, copyright 1940, renewed © 1968 by Sally Benson. Used by permission of Dial Books for Young Readers, a Division of Penguin Young Readers Group, a Member of Penguin Group (USA) Inc., 345 Hudson St., New York, NY 10014. All rights reserved.

The Story of Prometheus; The Adventures of Theseus; and Jason and the Golden Fleece— Line drawings by Willy Pogany, from *The Golden Fleece and the Heroes Who Lived Before Achilles* by Padraic Colum (New York: Macmillan, 1921)

While every care has been taken to trace and acknowledge copyright, the editors tender their apologies for any accidental infringement when copyright has proven untraceable. They would be pleased to include the appropriate acknowledgment in any subsequent edition of this publication.